The Pre-Raphaelite Trail In Sussex

·BIRD AULIS·
'The Mother and the monk bent down,
And lift her from the floor.

Peter Wise

S.B. Publications

DEDICATION
*This book is dedicated to my partner, Sally
and my two daughters, Verity and Isobel.*

First published in 2003 by S.B. Publications
19 Grove Road, Seaford, East Sussex BN25 1TP

ISBN 185770 267 0

Designed and Typeset by EH Graphics, East Sussex (01273) 515527

FRONT COVER: SHOWS BY WILLIAM HOLMAN HUNT (BY PERMISSION OF
WORTHING MUSEUM AND ART GALLERY) WAR MEMORIAL IN BOLNEY CHURCH,
DETAIL OF STAINED GLASS WINDOW IN KINGSTON CHURCH (PHOTOS BY THE
AUTHOR) AND STANDEN (BY KIND PERMISSION OF THE NATIONAL TRUST)

TITLE PAGE: 'BIRD AULIS' BY A. MORGAN PRICE - BY PERMISSION OF WORTHING
MUSEUM AND ART GALLERY

BACK COVER: EDWARD BURNE-JONES' SEASIDE RETREAT AT ROTTINGDEAN (PHOTO
BY THE AUTHOR) AND 'WINCHELSEA CHURCH 'BY WALTER CRANE (BY PERMISSION
OF WORTHING MUSEUM AND ART GALLERY).

Contents

'DR. EDWARD WILSON AS A BOY' BY WILLLAM HOLMAN HUNT - PERMISSION OF WORTHING MUSEUM AND ART GALLERY

The Author

Peter Wise is an art historian with a particular interest in how the topography and countryside of Britain has inspired many artists over the years. He is married, has two children and lives in Sussex where he has been all his life. As well as writing he works within the National Health Service. He is a member of the William Morris Society and the Pre-Raphaelite Society.

The author is most grateful to the rectors and vicars of all the churches concerned as well as to the many professionals, academics and other individuals who provided invaluable help and assistance with this book.

The author has checked the information contained in this book and believes it to be correct, and cleared copyright if appropriate. If however there is an unforeseen infringement in copyright the author apologises for this.

The author welcomes comments about this book from readers, in particular any new information about the subjects discussed. Email: peterrwise@yahoo.com

Introduction

The Pre-Raphaelites: a term that still resonates with art lovers today and probably for many different reasons. It conjures up various responses: love, hate, romance and intrigue, to name but a few. It might also mean rebellion, beauty, madness and sensuality to others, or even, on a more practical level, an association with interior decoration. Some might consider it to represent the cutting edge of Victorian art, or simply a rather backward looking group of artists with a passion for medieval times.

Images brought to the fore by the mention of 'Pre-Raphaelite' might include the prostrate figure of *Ophelia*, the Shakespearian character, drowning in a river of symbolic flora (modelled by Elizabeth Siddal and actually partly painted in Surrey). Another picture brought to mind might be of sheep grazing on a cliff top, that have been painted so meticulously, that they are almost photographic (in a work called *Our English Coasts* by Holman Hunt, that was largely completed in Sussex). Other favourites might be subjects from a mythical past, inhabited by knights and fair damsels, or simply beautiful, voluptuous depictions of women.

The names of Rossetti, Burne-Jones, Morris and Millais might spring to mind, with their interests in King Arthur, Keats and Tennyson amongst so many others.

This book explores how these artists and many other associates of the Pre-Raphaelites, had connections with Sussex throughout their lives, as well as highlighting their legacy, including the paintings they worked on in the county, the many beautiful examples of stained glass to be seen, and the houses where they stayed, lived, loved and worked. It introduces the reader to the principal personalities of the movement with particular reference to the times they were in Sussex.

HOW TO USE THIS BOOK

The latter part of the book includes fifteen trails that the interested traveller can follow in order to see the range of wonderful work inspired by the Pre-Raphaelites. These include houses open to the public, such as Standen, Petworth House and Batemans. There are also trips to the many churches that reflect the genius of Morris & Co. and associates. In addition, other Victorian artists and designers and the ensuing Arts and Crafts and Art Nouveau movements, which drew much of their inspiration from the Pre-Raphaelites, are explored.

Those visitors short of time are directed to trails 1, 2, 8, 10 and 12 which contain most of the main sights to be seen, although of course much of the enjoyment associated with these excursions, revolves around the discovery of a little known and unfamiliar 'gem', not to be found in many of the standard texts on the subject.

The map of Sussex at the end of the gazetteer section of the book shows the starting points for all fifteen trails. Directional instructions are given throughout the trails (in italics) and whilst it is possible to complete the trails using just these, readers will find a copy of the East or West Sussex Ordnance Survey Street Atlas to be useful. In addition, the Ordnance Survey Explorer and Landranger map series provide a further overview of the areas covered.

All the churches visited in this book are rated for their importance, nature of their contents and overall atmosphere on a one to five star rating. Simply, the more the stars, the better.

CHURCHES

The churches in the county, whether they be medieval in origin or Victorian, provide a unique chance, outside of the galleries and country houses, to view the work of artists and designers from the nineteenth century.

William Morris glass is well represented in ecclesiastical buildings throughout Sussex, with an important early commission for Morris, Marshall, Faulkner & Co. being their work at the Church of St. Michael and All Angels in Brighton.

There is more relatively early work to be seen at another Brighton church(The Annunciation)and at Haywards Heath. After 1875, Morris had control of the firm and a fine example of his mid-period glass designed principally by Burne-Jones, can be found at Rotherfield. The village church at Rottingdean contains some stunning examples of Burne-Jones' later style in the windows that celebrate the marriage of his daughter, Margaret. There are also many less important Morris windows in the area, such as those at Rye, Wadhurst and Brighton College. Some of these incorporate designs that were first used elsewhere in the country and were perhaps adapted for later use and a number are the work of John Henry Dearle who became the chief designer of stained glass for Morris & Co. following the deaths of Morris and Burne-Jones. There is even a window in St. Giles' church at Dallington designed by Dearle's son, Duncan and dating from 1950.

Sussex is also extremely lucky in having the only two churches to contain Morris painted tiles in the whole of the country. These are to be found within a few miles of one another near Worthing.

The degree to which artists associated with the Pre-Raphaelites influenced those around them can be appreciated by the way that images closely connected to them can be seen in an adapted form in a number of churches. For example there are several interpretations of Holman Hunt's *Light of the World* to be seen in glass, ranging from those quite closely inspired (Burpham) to others which are stylistically very different (Mayfield). There are also mosaic plaques quite clearly derived from paintings by Burne-Jones and G.F. Watts (Bolney and Selham respectively).

The work of C.E. Kempe is everywhere in Sussex and the quality does vary, but there are stunning examples of his work at Turners Hill, Fletching, Lavant and Ovingdean as well as two churches where his glass is omnipresent (St. Andrews' at Worthing and Danehill). There is also a beautiful and rare painted ceiling by him at Cuckfield.

Other stained glass designers and companies were inspired by the Pre-Raphaelites at various times and places, including the work of Heaton, Butler & Bayne at Seaford and Clayton & Bell at Lowfield Heath where the architect of the church was William Burges. The glass by the firm Powells is impressive, particularly at Oving near Chichester and the work of their leading designer, Henry Holiday at St. Michael's, Lewes.

Later work by designers associated with the Arts and Crafts Movement can be admired at Ticehurst (Christopher Whall), Boxgrove (Margaret Lowndes), and Little Horsted (Eleanor Brickdale).

The sheer quantity and range of church artefacts associated with the Pre-Raphaelites and those people inspired by these artists, mean that there are many visits made to these atmospheric buildings in the gazetteer section of this book.

VIEW TO THE BURNE - JONES HOME AT ROTTINGDEAN FROM THE CHURCHYARD - PHOTO BY AUTHOR

The Pre-Raphaelite Brotherhood

In the middle of the nineteenth century, British art was in a poor state. Portraiture and landscape painting were popular, but the typical examples of work produced in the schools and academies of art, were tired in execution, even comatose.

Against this background, the Pre-Raphaelite Brotherhood was formed in London in 1848, as a secret society of seven members who were all artists, or their associates. The founding members were William Holman Hunt, John Everett Millais and Dante Gabriel Rossetti. These three men were all a year either side of twenty and students at the Royal Academy, but they all felt out of step with the established art practice of the day. They were also three very different characters. Hunt had an intense drive and phenomenal determination, whereas Millais was the handsome, naturally gifted craftsman and Rossetti, a charismatic poet with a magnetic personality. However, together they constituted a powerful force for change.

The name 'Pre-Raphaelite' has over the years come to mean a whole range of differing styles of art, as well as an overall concept, but its original use was quite specific. Hunt, Millais and Rossetti felt that British art was in decline and in fact were critical of most art produced after the late works of the Renaissance painter, Raphael. After expressing this view to fellow students at the Royal Academy, their colleagues dubbed them the 'Pre-Raphaelites' which the three agreed was an accurate description. They then adopted this name as a means of protesting against the decadence into which they considered art had sunk, since the time of Raphael. The idea of having a secret society as a means of introducing change, was mainly Rossetti's, as was the use of the initials P.R.B. on their paintings, a practice that caused no little controversy.

One reason why art lacked inspiration was the way that institutions such as the Academy, followed long established traditions of placing artists of the sixteenth and seventeenth centuries on a pedestal. Their paintings were seen as the ideal, and the direct line back to the glories of the Renaissance. The trouble was that by the mid-nineteenth century, much of the work being completed was drained of real meaning and was just a pale imitation of the art of previous centuries. Hunt's impassioned cry was *'to do battle against the frivolous art of the day'* by which he meant this bland copying of works with a historical subject, as well as in the popular genre subjects and pictures of everyday life. The Brotherhood wanted to paint more serious subjects and to use full colour and greater luminosity, so breaking away from the established code of the time. They wanted to work directly from nature rather than from the style of previous artists, and to do this they would take the highly unconventional step of working out of doors. Of course, this innovation was also being explored in France and would lead to other tumultuous changes in art with the arrival of Impressionism.

Rossetti, Millais and Hunt asked four people to join them in their quest, who are less well known figures today, but nevertheless still important to the story. There was James Collinson, briefly a painter and also for a while the intended husband to Gabriel's sister, the poet Christina Rossetti. He later became a priest. Then there was Gabriel's brother, William who although never really a practising artist, performed a nevertheless vital role, as the chronicler of the movement. He was in addition, a writer and critic on artistic matters, as was Frederic George Stephens, the penultimate member of the Brotherhood. Finally, there was Thomas Woolner, who became a successful sculptor after a brief spell of emigration to Australia. It was this group of individuals that constituted the mystical number of seven members.

There were strong influences on which the group drew and these were primarily the views of two men, the art critic John Ruskin, and a painter of an earlier generation, Ford Madox Brown. In addition, the actual art that was produced (and could be seen)prior to the time of Raphael, had enormous impact on the newly formed Brotherhood. Into this melting pot of ideas went other vital beliefs, such as the need for serious subject matter including the dominant stories from the Bible and only slightly less importantly, Shakespeare. But there was also a desire to comment on their own times in the choice of contemporary subjects. So, in this year of revolutions in France, Italy and Germany, the PRB was set to cause its own revolution within artistic circles.

Although the Brotherhood itself would only exist for a few years the influence of The Pre-Raphaelites would be felt well into the next century. Many later artists would be inspired in varying ways by its radical ideas.

The Pre-Raphaelite Sisterhood

In recent years more attention has been paid to the role of women in the development of the Pre-Raphaelite style. The idea of a 'sisterhood' relates more to the overall influence of women artists to the development of the style than to a particular group of women that came together at a specific time. Many of these women were better known as the models, mistresses or wives of the men associated with the movement, but they were also accomplished artists in their own right. Examples would include Lizzie Siddal, Maria Zambaco, Marie Spartali (later Stillman) and Evelyn De Morgan. In addition, the daughters or sisters of men such as Madox Brown, William Morris, Frederick Sandys and George Price Boyce have until recently, been commented on more for their familial connections than for their artistic prowess.

Rossetti and Lizzie Siddal met two other significant female artists now associated with Pre-Raphaelitism in 1854, whilst staying at Scalands Farm near Robertsbridge in Sussex. They were Barbara Leigh Smith (later Bodichon) and Anna Mary Howitt. They (together with Rossetti) made similar but distinctly different sketches of Lizzie at that time. Despite being prolific artists for a number of years, until recently Bodichon was better known as a pioneering champion of women's rights whilst Howitt was virtually unknown. Siddal's own considerable talent was, until the last fifteen years or so, obscured by the fascination with her tempestuous relationship with Rossetti and events surrounding her early death.

Rossetti's sister, Christina, has perhaps eclipsed her brother's reputation as a poet, but even so her contributions towards early Pre-Raphaelite ventures such as the magazine *The Germ* have not received the recognition they deserve.

The gazetteer section of this book also includes a visit to a church containing glass by Eleanor Fortescue Brickdale. Born in 1872 she completed work that was a celebration of the early work of the Brotherhood, but her skills as a painter, illustrator and stained glass designer are still relatively unknown.

DETAIL FROM A STAINED GLASS WINDOW DESIGNED BY ELEANOR FORTESCUE BRICKDALE AT LITTLE HORSTED CHURCH - PHOTO BY AUTHOR

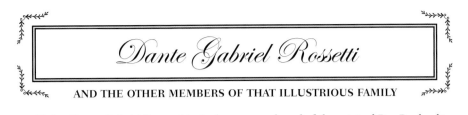

Dante Gabriel Rossetti

AND THE OTHER MEMBERS OF THAT ILLUSTRIOUS FAMILY

Today, Dante Gabriel Rossetti is the best remembered of the original Pre-Raphaelite group, perhaps because of his intriguing and well discussed personal life, as much as for the legacy of his art and poetry. He is also arguably, the Pre-Raphaelite artist who has the most documented connections to Sussex.

Gabriel was born on May 12th 1828 at 38, Charlotte Street, London, where nearby and ten years later, Millais would live when he and his parents first arrived in London from Jersey. Gabriel was the second of four children born in successive years. The eldest of his siblings was Maria, and William and Christina were his younger brother and sister respectively. All of the Rossetti children would achieve some degree of fame during their lives.

Their father was an Italian exile, a 'larger than life figure' who told fantastic tales of narrowly escaping his home country and fleeing to England. He was talking at a time when there was a changing political climate in Italy, and because of his allegiances to Napoleon, Rossetti Snr. had needed to disappear quickly, on board a ship skippered by an English admiral.

His wife Frances, was half Italian and half English, and her own father told an equally amazing tale. Apparently he saw the Bastille stormed during the French Revolution whilst being employed as the secretary to a close associate of the monarchy. He had a bloodied sword thrust into his hand by one of the crowd, but rapidly gave it away to someone else and made his escape. Frances, like her husband was not a conventional Victorian, and the relaxed and creative atmosphere at home, enabled the Rossetti children to develop their natural talents.

Christened Gabriel Charles Dante Rossetti, the eldest son later wished to be known as Dante Gabriel, which no doubt made him feel closer to his great hero, the fourteenth century poet, Dante Alighieri. Many of his paintings and drawings are based on works such as *Vita Nuova* and *The Divine Comedy*, by the great Italian writer.

Gabriel's school life was relatively uneventful and when he left, he had no real idea of how he wished to spend his life. In fact, there is a story of how he considered becoming a telegraph operator, (told by Holman Hunt, when years later, a memorial to Rossetti was unveiled on the Chelsea Embankment) a career option which fortunately came to nothing. The tale goes that whilst being shown the simplicity of the job he nevertheless said that *'it would be absolutely useless for me to undertake the work. I could not do it.'*

In reality, he spent some comparatively idle years at an art academy called Sass's,(where he received tuition from the same teacher as Millais before him) and it is during this period that his parents were staying at **9 High Street, Hastings.** Rossetti Snr. was recuperating after a severe bout of bronchitis and it was the usual Victorian practice, both during and after illness, to take the sea air.

Three years later, Gabriel entered the Antique School of the Royal Academy in Piccadilly, still pondering if he wished to devote his time to poetry or painting. Although critical of the teaching methods there - he once described the past President of the Academy, Sir Joshua Reynolds as *'Sloshua'* (slosh referring to the sombre tones of the

NO. 9 HIGH STREET HASTINGS - PHOTO BY AUTHOR

paintings then in vogue), he did of course meet some fellow students who were to change the direction of his life.

During the next two years Gabriel became acquainted with Hunt, Ford Madox Brown, Millais and Thomas Woolner who all shared his vision of a new form of art. After effectively using Hunt and Brown as tutors, the Brotherhood was formed and Gabriel commenced his first important oil, *The Girlhood of Mary Virgin* which was to contain the mysterious initials PRB.

At the same time, his sister Maria was working as a translator before becoming a governess for a relative of the Marchioness of Bath, for whom her Aunt Charlotte already worked. William was to be employed as a clerk in the Excise Office and Christina was also required to earn a living and with a view to this was learning French and Italian.

In August 1848, Mrs. Rossetti and her husband, together with William and Christina were at *'dreary snobbish **Brighton***'. That was how Gabriel described the town in a letter to his brother sent from London. Christina and Maria had been staying in the town prior to being joined by other members of the family, and Maria had been in the sea with the help of a bathing machine. Before Maria returned home, they both decreed that the pier was similarly dreary! Gabriel wrote of having made a study for the colour of his picture and also a nude study for the figure of St. Anne, who appears in the painting with her daughter, the Virgin Mary. His mother was the model for St. Anne in the final work, so perhaps this is a reference to a preliminary study for the figure!

A year later, the painting was exhibited and then sold, to the Dowager Marchioness of Bath, probably with the assistance of Gabriel's Aunt Charlotte. Gabriel initially received sixty guineas for it but increased this to eighty, apparently by using his charm.

Gabriel also mentions in his letter, that he was reading a recently published book on the poet, John Keats and calls him *'a glorious fellow'*- he was another great source of inspiration to the young painter. Whilst staying in Brighton, William wrote some of his sonnets which would later appear in *The Germ* and Christina dashed off several poems. *The Germ* was the magazine of the Brotherhood dedicated to spreading their views on art as well as reproducing their etchings and poetry.

Christina returned to **Brighton** in August 1850 with Maria, staying at **34 West Street.** These two visits form part of a number of stays in seaside resorts used by Rossetti family members for convalescence. In the same year, James Collinson had called off his proposed marriage to Christina and at the same time, left the Brotherhood. Undoubtedly her mood whilst in the town was likely to have been downbeat. She wrote to brother William reminding him of local sights they had both seen a couple of years before, - *'Yesterday walking up Western Street I recognised the familiar shop of Pratt, Hairdresser;'* but further on in the letter makes an almost casual but painful reference to her circumstances, - *'I wish you would find out whether Mr. Collinson is as delicate as he used to be'.* Interestingly in October, William wrote for the first time about Charles Bagot Cayley, who after much reticence later became Christina's second and last serious suitor.

1850 was also the year Gabriel met Elizabeth Siddal for the first time. She was of course the archetypal pale, red haired Pre- Raphaelite 'stunner'. Their relationship lasted over ten years, was frequently surrounded by pain and illness and has today become very much the subject of myth. Lizzie, as she was known, has represented different ideals to successive generations, and quite recently in the sixties, was an icon of the sexual revolution. In the seventies her importance historically was championed by the feminists, and whatever the viewpoint, she continues to be a figure of fascination up to the present day.

Before she met Gabriel, Lizzie worked as a milliner's assistant in a part of London called Cranbourne Alley. This was an area where men were prone to frequent, looking for women of easy virtue. Occasionally one of these men was the Irish poet, William Allingham who was a friend of the artists associated with the Pre-Raphaelites. One of this group of artists was Walter Deverell who was keen to find a red haired model for a painting based on Shakespeare's *Twelfth Night*, The story goes that with some help from Allingham and his own mother, Deverell managed to persuade Lizzie to sit for the picture and in the course of a later conversation, excitedly told Hunt and

NO. 34 WEST STREET BRIGHTON - PHOTO BY AUTHOR

Gabriel about her. It is said that Gabriel fell instantly in love with Lizzie the first time they met. Certainly he was annoyed when Hunt, tongue in cheek, announced to a mutual friend that Lizzie was his bride! As Gabriel and Lizzie got to know one another, she began to know more people associated with the group and to model for other painters. A famous example being when she sat for Millais's *Ophelia*.

This famous painting shows the Shakespearean character lying in a stream, and in order to achieve naturalistic effect, Millais suggested that Lizzie should lie in a bath, but with lamps underneath to keep the water warm. He is said to have been so involved in his work that he did not notice the lamps had gone out, which resulted in her becoming cold and she subsequently developed a severe chill. Millais had to promise Lizzie's father that he would pay her doctor's bills in order to avoid legal action over this.

There have been suggestions that Gabriel and Lizzie were engaged as early as 1851-2 but there is no definite certainty that they were ever engaged. Undoubtedly his feelings for her were more than just those of friendship, but already he was idolising her in a distant way, something that was to prove a stumbling block to the development of their relationship. Lizzie's health was never strong and as early as 1852 she was convalescing at **Hastings** and a couple of years later, she returned to rest at an inn there, in the company of Gabriel. He wrote to his mother to say that they were both going to move to a Mrs. Elphick's, at **5 High Street** in May of 1854. The rent was going to be 8s.; a cheaper price. In their front upstairs room, Gabriel drew several fine exquisite studies of Lizzie which show the increasing intimacy between the two lovers. He also wrote to say that the day after, they were planning to visit a Barbara Leigh Smith at **Robertsbridge,** with whom earlier they had gone for a walk through Hastings. This is the friend later to be Barbara Bodichon, an artist and early feminist who founded a women's university college at Cambridge. Her brother owned a farm called **Scalands** near the village, a place that Gabriel was to frequent on a number of subsequent occasions, sometimes in the company of Jane Morris. But that was in the future and in May of 1854 the weather in Hastings was described by Gabriel as *'delicious'* with the sea looking like *'enamel'* in the sun, and perhaps because of this he was considering asking William his brother, to send some *'painting-things'* from his rooms in London.

In another letter of the same month the situation in the town was *'rather slow here, and generally very windy, though often (there is) glorious sunlight'*. Gabriel suggested his friend, Allingham could come down for a day or so, and even gave travelling advice- *'his best plan would be to take a return ticket on Saturday, which costs £1 (second class), and will bring him back by the last train on Monday.'*

Gabriel and 'Guggums' (as he nicknamed Lizzie), did indeed go to Scalands and planned to visit *'several places tolerably within range hereabouts'* although Lizzie was not capable of much exercise. On this first visit, Gabriel is said to have mistaken the many hop kilns for small private chapels, subsequently thinking the local population were very religious! It was also at this time that Gabriel sold a water-colour called *Dante drawing an Angel* for £50, a price that he was overjoyed at.

Three days later the weather was *'decidedly warm'* and a Dr. Hale advised Lizzie to leave the Old Town in **Hastings** and go nearer the sea. It seems that Barbara had been investigating the possibility of Lizzie going into a sanatorium in Harley Street, London and was in contact with a *'relative'* of hers about this. The 'relative' was possibly none other than Florence Nightingale, before she left for the Crimea. It has been muted that Lizzie suffered from a curvature of the spine, but her illness is more likely to have been of a psychosomatic origin.

NO. 5 HIGH STREET HASTINGS - PHOTO BY AUTHOR

On a second visit to **Scalands** in mid-May, Gabriel made many sketches of Lizzie, which were very informal, sometimes depicting her drawing and all showing a great closeness between artist and sitter. During this time and despite her illness, Lizzie worked at a design for her composition called *Clerk Saunders*, the subject of a Scottish ballad. On one occasion the lovers scratched their initials on a pane of glass at the farm.

But Gabriel grew increasingly lethargic and again found things slow with a lack of *'tin'* (money) being an additional problem. At Hastings he found *'most wonderful things to paint, (but) I do not mean to paint a single one, as the pursuit of art is a bore, except when followed in the dozing style'*. So he strolled about the cliffs and shore or lay in the sun. Lizzie sometimes went with him, and he once drew a gypsy girl as she was an *'image of savage active health'* which might explain something about his mixed feelings towards Lizzie. Often, the couple would carve their initials on the cliffs or on ruins, although as time passed, Lizzie spent much of the time drawing. Gabriel's apathy continued and he wrote to Allingham of *'dense fogs of heat'* and how he wished a street crier would sell his *'plagues and the skeletons of one's house without reserve'*. Clearly his moods were up and down and this might explain his ambivalence about marriage. On his return to London, the familiarity of his surroundings enabled Gabriel to write several sonnets in quick succession.

It was about this period that John Ruskin, the influential art critic began to vigorously support the work of the Pre-Raphaelite Brotherhood, He was also keen to be an advocate for Lizzie's work, which might also have provided him with an escape from his own personal dilemmas. After all, his marriage was coming to an end, with his wife, Effie taking up with Millais. This was to prove to be one of the major scandals of Victorian society.(see chapter on Millais)

In the summer of 1855 Christina and her mother were convalescing in **Hastings** and Gabriel wrote to them there. Sounding rather romantic, he wondered if they were walking the same hills *'which grow rather monotonous'*, and related where he and Lizzie scratched their initials a year earlier. It was on East Hill *'where there is something which looks far off like a ruin'* but proves, *if I remember rightly, to be nothing but a blocked up door of some kind'*. He also wrote of a stone used for their initials at **Old Roar** which was a *'pretty place indeed and not very far'*. Gabriel and Lizzie were later to spend some time in Paris during this year, and this must have provided a change of environment from the more restrained delights of Hastings.

In 1856 Gabriel met Burne-Jones and William Morris who were studying at Oxford, which of course led later to the creation of the Firm subsequently known as Morris & Co. It also led to him meeting Jane Burden, Morris's future wife and Gabriel's second great flame. A few months later, Gabriel was instrumental in getting his friends and associates together to work on a common task. He was asked by an architect friend of Ruskin to do murals for the Oxford Union Debating Hall (now the library). This enterprise involved a whole group of artists that Gabriel gathered together. He enlisted Burne-Jones and Morris, as well as other artists of a similar mind including, Val Prinsep, Spencer Stanhope and a John Hungerford Pollen, who was the only one with any experience of doing frescos. The poet Coventry Patmore was also present and he would afterwards praise the murals.

This venture may well have been a welcome distraction from Lizzie, as they had disagreed and she was with her cousin in Sheffield. Their relationship was in confusion-Lizzie could not be his mistress if she was later to be Gabriel's wife. However once again they made up and he later joined her at Matlock in the Peak District.

THE FISHING QUARTER AND CLIFFS IN HASTINGS - PHOTO BY AUTHOR

Two years passed and Gabriel's seven stained glass panels (shown at the International Exhibition) of the 'Parable of the Vineyard' led to the Firm's commissions for glass at a number of churches including **St. Michael & All Angels** in **Brighton**. Some people even believed these panels were medieval. Against the background of Gabriel's increasing success and prosperity, Lizzie's health continued to decline. Morris married Jane Burden and they had Philip Webb build and design the Red House for them at Bexleyheath in Kent. Burne-Jones was also set to wed Georgiana MacDonald.

In this atmosphere of marital betrothal, in April 1860, Lizzie summoned Gabriel to meet her in **Hastings.** He wrote to Madox Brown afterwards expressing enormous concern for her well being - *'she has been ready to die daily and more than once a day'.* Then on the thirteenth of the month he sent a letter to his mother from **12 East Parade, Hastings** saying *'I write you this word to say that Lizzy and I are going to be married at last, in as few days as possible'.* It has been cruelly suggested that Gabriel (at least sub-consciously) knew that a marriage to Lizzie would be a short thing due to her ailing health. He also seems to have been pre-occupied with how not marrying her would influence his own well being. Four days later in a letter to his brother William he says *'if I were to lose her now, I do not know what effect it might have on my mind'* and he laments the delay in marrying Lizzie due to her continued poor health. Lizzie was suffering- *'she has taken some slight things -such as beef tea and jelly without as yet bringing them up again'.* The delay could however also indicate some ambivalence on the part of Lizzie. Gabriel even contemplates obtaining a special license *'as there seems little prospect of her being able as yet to enter the cold church with safety'.* His letters to the family in London do not invite them to the forthcoming ceremony and are less than joyous in tone. Lizzie's ill health delayed the wedding for another month and it is possible that the vomiting and stomach upsets she experienced were aggravated by her increasing dependence on the drug, laudanum. This is similar in many of its characteristics to opium and was used widely for vague medicinal reasons by the Victorians. It had been prescribed by one of Lizzie's doctors a number of years before and was to play a significant role, as shall be seen, in later events.

However, on the 23rd. May 1860 with no friends or family present, the couple were finally married in **St. Clement's Church** in **Hastings.** Two strangers signed the witness book, and they may well have been the church caretaker and his wife. Gabriel wrote a brief note to his mother saying *'Lizzie and I are just back from the church. We are going to Folkestone today hoping to get on to Paris if possible, but you will be grieved to hear her health is no better as yet.'* Surprisingly, despite various ups and downs their honeymoon went well and perhaps some of the bitterness and resentments of recent years was forgotten, albeit for a short time.

They returned to London some three weeks later, but not before Gabriel had produced a drawing entitled *'How they met Themselves'.* This rather ominously shows a young couple meeting their own ghosts and is associated with the premonition of death. It certainly may shed some light on Gabriel's pre-occupations and his vision of what the future might hold. Gradually however the couple began to socialise and met with Burne-Jones and Georgiana who had themselves married on the 9th June. Other acquaintances were renewed including those with the poet Algernon Swinburne and the artists Frederick Sandys, Henry Holiday and Simeon Solomon all called. These young men each had a role to play in the expansion of the original Pre-Raphaelite ideas. At this time the Morris's were still living at Red House and the three couples would frequently meet there. When Georgina first met Lizzie she pronounced her to be *'as beautiful as imagination, poor thing',*

THE SEAHOUSES AREA IN HASTINGS WHERE GABRIEL AND LIZZIE STAYED (SEPARATELY) PRIOR TO THEIR WEDDING - PHOTO BY AUTHOR

Although July saw Lizzie once again at **Brighton** for facilitate a 'cure' for her breathing difficulties and poor appetite, at the beginning of 1861 she found herself pregnant and shone with renewed health. Later the same year she was at Hastings taking the air but tragically the baby was stillborn shortly afterwards.

Lizzie never really recovered from this event and in February of 1862 she was found dying by a distraught Gabriel when he returned to their home at 14 Chatham Place, London. The cause of her death is of course still the subject of much debate- some people have suggested it was suicide, whilst others consider the most likely reason to be an accidental overdose of laudanum, which she had been taking in ever increasing quantity. However, it is likely she left a note asking for her vulnerable brother to be looked after, which suggests her intent and perhaps also some animosity towards Gabriel whose name was not mentioned. A week later, she was buried at Highgate cemetery where Gabriel famously deposited the book of his own poems in the coffin with Lizzie's body, as he felt they had been worked on whilst Lizzie had been suffering and unwell.

The other members of the Rossetti household spent time with Gabriel in the days that followed no doubt to offer as much support as possible. Christina was now close to becoming a successful poet having completed her best known work, *Goblin Market,* almost three years before (it was published only a fortnight after Lizzie's funeral). Maria had joined the religious community, All Saints, based in Margaret Street in London, and Christina was an associate of another religious order. Michael bravely continued to bring home much needed monies from the Excise Office.

The shock of Lizzie's death made Gabriel withdraw and he moved to new accommodation at Cheyne Walk in Chelsea. There he was to eventually spend much of his time in the company of a whole menagerie of animals, some of them quite exotic.

ST. CLEMENTS CHURCH IN HASTINGS - PHOTO BY AUTHOR

The next five years were to be very successful for Gabriel. He prolifically produced work for lucrative commissions and even contributed to an important book devoted to William Blake in 1863. He had been friendly with its author Alexander Gilchrist and when he suddenly died of scarlatina, Gabriel stepped in to help his widow complete the book.

January of that year saw Christina Rossetti at **81 High Street Hastings** because of her delicate health, just as Lizzie had sought the recuperative qualities of that town before her. She had her cousin Henrietta Polydore with her, who was suffering from consumption. In between bouts of illness, Christina worked on proofs of a new edition of *Goblin Market*. It is around this time that she was attracted to Charles Bagot Cayley, a brilliant linguist and translator who had appeared in a couple of Ford Madox Brown's pictures as a young man. He was also rather eccentric and undemonstrative, but the last great love of Christina's life. He later proposed to her but was rejected, for unclear reasons (it might have been his relative poverty, religious beliefs or the constraints of her own membership of a holy order). Nevertheless she remained great friends with him until his death in 1883 after which he was buried in **Hastings cemetery.** Christina made a special trip there in April 1884 to visit his grave and her poem One Sea-side Grave has been connected to this. If true, these lines give some idea of Christina's hidden emotions.

> 'Cold as the cold Decembers,
> Past as the days that set,
> While only one remembers

> *And all the rest forget, -*
> *But one remembers yet.'*

Also in 1865, William Morris had to sell the Red House because of a reduced income and he, Jane and their two daughters, Jenny and May, relocated to London. It was there that Jane began to sit regularly for Gabriel and the two of them became closer. It is also in this period that Jane's own health problems begin - she was also destined to suffer from ill defined maladies throughout her life.

By 1870 a love affair between Gabriel and Jane was becoming obvious to everyone who knew them. For a variety of possible reasons (even memories of his time there with Lizzie) Gabriel chose to go to Scalands again and stay in a new cottage loaned to him by Barbara Bodichon. She found his appearance greatly changed. He may have thought country living would help to ease his increasing insomnia, or that he might be able to see Jane out of the public eye. In addition, he was awaiting the imminent publication of the poems that his literary agent had recovered from Lizzie's grave. On an evening in early October 1868 he had arranged for her coffin to be opened, in order to retrieve the poems for publication. The book was thoroughly soaked and needed much disinfecting. There is also the story that Lizzie's hair was found to be as golden as when she had been alive. This infamous incident of disinterring the poems is to many people the moral lowpoint of Rossetti's life. He himself complained of increased paranoia, believing at the worse times that he had desecrated her resting place.

Gabriel was haunted by memories of Lizzie and his dark retrospective mood can be judged by a poem of the time called Barren Spring :-

> *'So Spring comes merry towards me here, but earns*
> *No answering smile from me, whose life is twin'd*
> *With the dead boughs that winter still must bind,*
> *And whom to-day the spring no more concerns.'*

He had to share the cottage at **Scalands** with an American journalist by the name of William Stillman. He was a widower who would later marry Marie Spartali who modelled for Gabriel and was a friend of Burne-Jones. She was also an accomplished painter herself having received some training from Madox Brown in her youth. Unfortunately Stillman suggested that Gabriel might try a sleeping drug called chloral hydrate to help his insomnia and although initially reluctant to take it he was later to grow reliant on it. The two men agreed to share the costs of residing at Scalands although Gabriel entertained a good deal more, inviting Madox Brown, and amongst others, the Morrises. It also meant that Gabriel could visit Jane at nearby **Hastings,** where she was staying with her daughters, suffering from a throat infection. Also, on the 27th. March he was visited by Morris and Jane about which he commented; *'Top (the nickname for Morris) and Jane are here today, the former insolently solid-the latter better than when I last saw her in Hastings'.* They went *'church crawling'* locally and Gabriel collected wild flowers which he sent to his mother. Jane visited alone on the 18th. April from which date they were together almost until the time Gabriel left on the 9th. May. He went because Barbara needed her cottage back but in view of the improvement in Gabriel's health, he tried to rent another house in the vicinity although in the end he never occupied this.

Throughout the latter part of his stay his mood was more buoyant and he worked at a number of sketches. He made a crayon drawing of Jane which he thought *'the best thing I ever did'.* He also commenced a portrait of Stillman and finished a drawing of the local gamekeeper's daughter, Sophy Burgess which earned him fifty guineas. He additionally did some preparatory work on the painting *Dante's Dream.* At the end of

his Sussex break his mood was certainly better as can be seen in the poem 'Fin de Maggio':-
'O May sits crowned with Hawthorn-flowers
And is Love's month they say
And love's the fruit that is ripened best
By ladies' eyes in May'

Morris came to pick up Jane at the end of her stay presumably for reasons of respectability and it was for the same reason that he and

Gabriel took a joint lease on the more famous location for Jane and Gabriel 's romances-Kelmscott.

Gabriel suffered a number of setbacks in the years before 1875 - he was attacked by critics for the explicit and sensuous nature of his poetry and this precipitated a major nervous illness. His relationship with Jane became more distant. His drug habit was also more established. These events in turn affected the health of other family members and Christina and her mother again sought recuperation through the country air of Sussex in 1872. This took the form of a farmhouse at **Glottenham** which is not far from Scalands.

THE HAYLEY FAMILY GRAVE IN HASTINGS CEMETERY - PHOTO BY AUTHOR

In 1873 Christina was again in the county, this time at **17 Robertson Terrace** in **Hastings.** She was accompanied by her mother and Henrietta Polydore, whose consumptive condition was now much worse. From the number of visits Christina made to the town it is easy to imagine the high opinion she had of Hastings. She wrote 'these lodgings are the nicest we ever took at the seaside; our large sitting room looks across a bit of green straight on to the sea'.

But bad news arrived- Maria had an attack of erysipelas and needed to spend time at the **All Saints Sisterhood Home** at **Eastbourne** in order to convalesce. Throughout all this sickness there was one piece of good news- William had been on a European tour in the company of Lucy Madox Brown (Brown's daughter) and on their return he proposed to Lucy and she accepted. On the whole this provided a positive boost to the other family members. They married the following year.

Around this time Gabriel was beginning one of his most familiar late works featuring Jane, the painting *Astarte Syriaca*. Before this was completed Gabriel left Kelmscott and October 1875 found him in Bognor, where he stayed for the next nine months.

He may have gone there at the suggestion of his friend, the minister and painter James Smetham, or to simply escape London for a while. He rented a secluded house called Aldwick Lodge on the seafront. The autumnal weather was wild and the wind caused the house to shake and disorientated cows strolled through the garden eating fallen leaves. Gabriel made himself go out for long walks with his dog, Dizzy and collected sea anemones and other marine life along the beach. Sometimes he was seen walking briskly towards Selsey Bay past ruined groynes and boulders by the sea. Occasionally he was visited by family and friends and at the end of November by Jane. She modelled for the painting and stayed until Christmas time. Morris was left at Kelmscott and complained that he was living on a pound of bacon and a tin of kangaroo meat! The model Alexa Wilding also came down and sat for the well known painting, 'The Blessed Damosel'. At one point Gabriel sought to escape the bad light and draughts and moved to a converted stable in the centre of Bognor. Here Jane returned to sit for him in March of 1876 with her daughter May, and it may have been around this time she made the decision that the liaison with Gabriel must cease. He was at the height of his addiction to chloral and this could have been the point at which she realised the extent of this. Additionally she had the welfare of her children to consider. Although they continued to meet after the time in Bognor it was there that their intense relationship effectively ended.

Meanwhile, Maria had completed her final vows for the All Saints Sisterhood and the summer of 1876 found Christina and her mother at **Eastbourne** to visit her.

Following another period of both physical and mental ill health for Gabriel, he and Jane recommenced their correspondence in 1877. Jane was also not so well and Gabriel was reminded of Lizzie by her shaky handwriting. In the winter of that year she went with the family to Italy as a warm climate had been recommended to her instead of the 'cures' by the British seaside. Gabriel wrote to her there mentioning the Scalands portrait and in 1879 was still working from it:- *'You remember my beginning a picture from the old head of you done at Scalands. I began it a second time (not liking the first thoroughly) and it is now well advanced. The head is like you I think as if done from nature, and is satisfactory in execution.'* The visit abroad proved to be less than

THE BEACH AT BOGNOR LOOKING TOWARDS SELSEY - PHOTO BY AUTHOR

successful-Morris developed gout and Jane collapsed in Venice. So in February 1880 she was back taking the 'cure' at **2 Carlisle Parade** in **Hastings.**

Christina had previously convalesced at **2 Gladstone Villas, Seaford** in July of 1879 and a year later she was in **Eastbourne** once again where she sent a letter dated 16th. July to Gabriel from an address at **111 Pevensey Road.** Mrs. Rossetti senior was convalescing with her daughter and Christina was not overly enamoured of the town. She wrote '*the horrors of this place would certainly overwhelm you, - its idlers, brass bands, nigger minstrels of British breed, and other attractions; but (when) more frivolous, am in a degree amused*'. Gabriel was at this time somewhat critical of the wisdom of a visit to the seaside. He says:- '*Certainly a sea beach so visited as you describe by wind and wave cannot be always an agreeable lounge.*' However Christina's health did rally a little afterwards.

The health of Maria was not improving- she had cancer and despite the caring attentions of members of the convent, she sadly died in late November. She was buried at Brompton cemetery in London, an occasion Christina wrote about shortly afterwards; '*Flowers covered her, loving mourners followed her, hymns were sung at her grave, and the sun (I vividly remember) made a miniature rainbow in my eyelashes*'.

During the years 1877-1881 Gabriel sought almost complete seclusion although he continued to work. His health was deteriorating and his drug addiction spiralling out of control. He was always glad to hear from Jane and she wrote to him from Italy in February 1881. Gabriel had written previously joking about the house that Burne-Jones had just bought in **Rottingdean**:- '*Ned was here the other evening. His style in conversation is getting beyond the pussy-cat and attaining the dicky-bird. No doubt you know he has bought a mansion near Brighton.*' Jane was less grating in her response:- '*I knew that Ned had a little place in Brighton, and a very wise thing too, the sea-air is the only thing that braces up the nerves.*'

October saw the publication of his last book - *Poems and Ballads* and the following February it was suggested that Gabriel went to the Westcliff bungalow at Birchington-on-Sea in Kent. Christina visited him there when she herself was well enough to do so and she was shocked at his physical decline. He was suffering from kidney poisoning caused by his long term use of chloral. Although he had periods of feeling better, his health was deteriorating. During a rare cliff walk, he reflected- '*It is beautiful, the world, and life itself. I am glad I have lived.*' He died on Easter Sunday. Christina and her mother were present at the time, the funeral taking place in the local church a few days later and described in her poem, *Birchington Churchyard.*

Four years later, Mrs Rossetti Snr, then over eighty and surprisingly healthy throughout her life also died. Although Christina appeared, on the surface, to cope well with another family loss, the following summer saw her sent to **Brighton** by her doctor in order to help her anxieties and frequent headaches. She took Olive, her eleven year old niece with her and they stayed at **17, Brunswick Road (Hove).** From there she wrote to William to say she felt better and that they had visited the Aquarium. This interlude was probably Christina's longest experience of being in the role of a mother.

In 1894 William's wife Lucy died from tuberculosis and Christina herself became increasingly ill with cancer. After so many years William finished his employment with the Inland Revenue but it was difficult to enjoy his more plentiful leisure time. Christina finally died on January 2nd. after a long painful illness. William was to live for a further 24 years and although surrounded by his four surviving children and friends, dealt with his grief by documenting the history of his family. One of the most fascinating of all Victorian families.

EASTBOURNE SEAFRONT IN VICTORIAN TIMES - PHOTO COURTESY OF STEVE BENZ

NO. 17 BRUNSWICK ROAD HOVE - PHOTO BY AUTHOR

William Holman Hunt

THE FAITHFUL PRE-RAPHAELITE

William Holman Hunt (1827-1910) is nowadays probably the least remembered of the three young men who back in 1848 met at the Royal Academy. With the similarly youthful Millais and Rossetti he formed the revolutionary set of like minds that came to be called the Pre-Raphaelite Brotherhood. They became firm friends with a unifying cause and common beliefs, but it was only Hunt who was to remain loyal to their ideals throughout his life.

'The Mad' (as he was affectionately known by Rossetti because of his tendency to work frantically like a maniac) was born in Cheapside, London on the 2nd. April 1827. He was named William Hobman after a rich uncle on his mother's side of the family, in the unlikely hope that one day he may become his heir. However, he later found out that his surname had been mis-spelt Holman on his certificate of baptism and chose thereafter to be known as Holman Hunt.

He was one of a relatively large family, having five sisters and a brother. His father, William Hunt was a manager of one of the many warehouses in the area and it was into this line of work that he expected his son to follow. He was however, also a keen amateur artist and from an early age the younger Hunt also showed an interest in and an aptitude for, painting and drawing. His father considered art to be a reasonable hobby and therefore did not discourage his son in his pursuits, but in no way did he think it could be a career. The boy even had a number of lessons from practising artists. On one occasion, he lost a camel hair brush that had been loaned to him by his father and looking desperately for a replacement, made a brush using his own camel coloured hair. Tied to a home made handle he presented this to his father who was somewhat amused, resulting in his son bursting into tears. Perhaps not the most sympathetic reception for one of his first creative efforts!

Hunt later attended boarding school and it was whilst there that he was visited by his wealthy uncle whose home was at Rectory Farm in Ewell, Surrey. Thus he was introduced to a part of the country which was to be an important backdrop to some of his most famous paintings.

After leaving school, he worked as a clerk to an auctioneer and as an assistant at a calico printers, but was fortunate in one important respect; his employers allowed him to continue to spend time working on his artistic interests. He also made regular visits to the nearby British Museum. It was also about this time he showed an early enthusiasm for the poetry of Keats which was to influence the choice of subject matter in his first paintings.

His father continued to be adamant that his son's future should be spent in the warehouse business and finally Hunt confronted him with the assertion that he had to become an artist and reluctantly this was understood. One of Hunt's favourite places of the time was Chingford church where he spent many hours painting and sketching (this was later the location for one of Arthur Hughes' finest works, *Home from the Sea*).

Hunt now made attempts to enter the Royal Academy, initially gaining day tickets from the Professor of Sculpture, Sir Richard Westmacott. After three attempts he was accepted as a probationer in July of 1844 and finally became a student in December of that year. He then met Millais who was stunning all around him with his prodigious talent and a close friendship developed between the two of them.

Hunt began to exhibit work from 1846 with strong contemporary moral themes. Other subject matter was based on The Bible, Shakespeare or Keats. He continued to read extensively and discovered the writings of Ruskin, in particular a volume of *Modern Painters* and began increasingly to be critical of contemporary art practice. These ideas were quickly disseminated to Millais and later Rossetti and others, leading to the formation of the Brotherhood in the autumn of 1848. The art establishment's angry reaction to this secret society was still to come.

After travelling to Paris and Belgium with Rossetti a year later, Hunt was again treading on the borders of Sussex in 1850. This is when he stayed at Knole Park near Sevenoaks, in Kent (now in the hands of The National Trust) with Rossetti and Stephens during October and November. He was working on his picture *Valentine Rescuing Sylvia from Proteus,* based on Shakespeare's play *Two Gentlemen of Verona.* In the work, Sylvia was modelled on Lizzie Siddal who had just been discovered by Walter Deverell and Rossetti. She was somewhat reluctant as Hunt had played a joke on her which she had not appreciated. She did not accompany them on the trip which was characterised, at least initially, by torrential rain on a daily basis. After a couple of months trying to paint the background to the picture 'a plein air', a damp Hunt returned to London. The finished work brims over with minute detail right down to the meticulously observed leaves and blades of grass. Hunt persevered longer than anyone else with the inclement weather and Rossetti's impatience with it, marks the decline of his interest in depicting nature so accurately.

KNOLE, SEVENOAKS IN KENT - BY KIND PERMISSION OF THE NATIONAL TRUST

The picture received a hostile reception when it was exhibited at the Royal Academy the next year, but gained a Liverpool Academy prize and was sold to a dealer.

Hunt continued to paint just outside Sussex in 1851, this time in Surrey. He was at Ewell, painting *The Hireling Shepherd* and *The Light of the World* in the company of Millais. The latter work was to finally give Hunt financial security and to become the most popular religious painting to be reproduced in the Victorian era and for many years thereafter.

In June of 1852 Hunt accepted a commission to paint the sheep that appear in the background of *The Hireling Shepherd* as a separate picture. He soon however persuaded his patron that this painting should be a new work and not just a copy. At this time Robert Martineau, a pupil of Hunt's, introduced him to the writer Edward Lear, now most remembered for his nonsense rhymes. Lear was also a keen artist who showed Hunt some pencil sketches he had been working on. These carried phonetic descriptions such as *'korn'*, *'rox'* and *'ski'* which were characteristic of Lear's personality. He wondered if Hunt could produce an oil from one of the sketches but instead Hunt invited him to come down to **Fairlight** where they might work together.

Lear offered to travel down and find accommodation and found some at Clive Vale farm (now gone) where Hunt and William Rossetti joined him a little later. On their arrival, Lear seemed rather guarded and suggested that they should divide up the house and just meet for meals. However they got on so well that this soon became a standing joke and it transpired that the well built Lear nevertheless had a profound fear of dogs. He had expected the other artists to arrive with perhaps, one of the Newfoundlands that Martineau's parents had at nearby Fairlight Lodge. Lear, for the life of him could not understand how anyone would wish to call there with such animals resident!

For the first week or so Lear and Hunt painted together by a cliff using the same landscape. At this time, Lear was working on his oil *The Quarries of Syracuse* and most of the time they enjoyed each others company, Lear taught Hunt some Italian and also wrote further *Nonsense Rhymes* between painting. Despite being twenty years older he called Hunt *'Daddy'* or *'Pa'* and acted like a son, writing down his advice on aspects of art in *'Ye Booke of Hunte'* for later perusal.

Millais then wrote to say he was going to come down and together the

STAINED GLASS WINDOW IN TILLINGTON CHURCH - PHOTO BY AUTHOR'

three of them visited **Winchelsea** and **Rye.** The weather at the time was fine but after a fortnight there was a violent storm and the weather on the day following was very misty. In his book describing the Brotherhood, there is a tale about a stranger who met Hunt on the cliff this day. He was a fellow artist and their conversation centred around the Pre-Raphaelites whom he assured Hunt did not work directly from nature but did everything in their studios! In addition he told Hunt that he personally knew them as well as he knew himself! Hunt seems to have taken all this in his stride even wondering what the stranger's response might be the next year when he saw *Our English Coasts* on the wall of the Royal Academy.

This is the painting that incorporated the sheep within its composition for the commission mentioned above. It is undoubtedly one of the key early Pre-Raphaelite works with its brilliant colours and minutely detailed finish. The work consists of numerous tiny strokes of colour showing the effect of light on different surfaces, a prime example being a sheep's ear where the individual veins can be delineated with the light coming from behind. The picture was very influential to a number of painters who wished to emulate its technique.

As with all of Hunt's work there is much symbolism to be found beneath the mesmerising formal qualities of the work. In 1860, F. G. Stephens suggested that the work could be taken as a satire on the anxieties of the time, that Napoleon III might invade the country (the sheep representing a diffident early Home Guard) and Hunt himself changed the painting's title to *Strayed Sheep* in order to emphasise its religious connotations of the flock, or people erring from the path of faith.

In November of the same year Hunt wrote to Rossetti from Fairlight, *'I hope to return on Thursday morning, there is only one more mornings work to be done to the sheep picture, the other I must spend on a small sketch I began some time ago for the torturer....'* This sketch is the work *Fairlight Downs - Sunlight on the Sea.* The 'torturer' mentioned was Hunt's dentist although he never did give the work to him as payment for professional services. In fact, Hunt appears to have had some difficulty finishing the work as he returned to Fairlight in July 1856 with it, whilst recuperating from an attack of malaria. The intervening years had been very busy and although Hunt had become financially secure he had spent long periods of time in the Middle East living rather dangerously. Also, his father had just died as well as Thomas Seddon, the artist who had accompanied Hunt on his travels. He probably continued to work on *Fairlight Downs* when he returned to the studio he shared with Michael Halliday in London. He was back again in Sussex two years later when he wrote to Lear to say that he was completing the work and also commencing another work, *The School-girl's Hymn.*

Fairlight Downs is essentially a landscape picture which has a harsh contrast between the sunlit sea and a land in shade, something for which it was criticised when it was exhibited. It contains no human figure but there is a dog chasing a walking stick, which interestingly is thought to be Caesar, one of Martineau's dogs that so upset Lear.

The School-girl's Hymn has in its background a similar landscape to the previous painting and shows Miriam Wilkinson, the daughter of a labourer who came to Hunt's studio in Kensington to sit. Hunt was to stay another two weeks at Fairlight in August 1859 to do more work on the painting whilst feeling stressed and staying at the Martineau home. He may even have come back again in 1860 for more revisions. The painting also has a connection to a poem by Coventry Patmore although it is not a direct illustration of this but a saleable genre picture.

At this time Hunt's contact with Sussex effectively ends although he may well have visited **Brighton** and the neighbourhood in 1860. Of course many of Hunt's important paintings were completed in The Holy Land and it was undoubtedly the need to work on major works such as *The Finding of the Saviour in the Temple* that delayed the completion of the two latter works painted mainly in the Fairlight area.

In 1861, Thomas Woolner proposed marriage to Fanny, the eldest daughter of George Waugh, a successful chemist (a later and more famous member of the family was the novelist, Evelyn Waugh). Hunt and Woolner had been visiting the family for some while but Fanny found Hunt the more attractive and so rejected Woolner's offer. Woolner later married her younger sister, Alice and after this marriage Hunt found himself at Burton Park near **Petworth** in order to complete a portrait of the patron Thomas Fairbairn's wife and children at their home. It seems that the atmosphere at Petworth was rather dull and Hunt's thoughts turned increasingly to his own needs for a partner.

On the 28th. December 1865 he married Fanny Waugh and the next year with his wife pregnant they embarked on a tour of the Far East. They were delayed at Florence because of quarantine regulations and it was there that their son Cyril was born on the 26th. October. Tragically, Fanny contracted malaria and died on the 20th. December. Grief stricken, Hunt returned to England with his son and slowly began painting again, his work included a portrait of his sister-in-law Edith, Fanny's younger sister. In June 1868 he returned to Florence and it was at this time he painted the portrait of *Bianca* which made the now besotted Edith wild with jealousy (see **Worthing** trail). Hunt knew that any potential relationship with Edith would be opposed by her parents particularly as marriage to a deceased wife's sister was then illegal. Consequently the couple finally 'tied the knot' in November 1875 at Neuchatel, Switzerland because there was no such problems under Swiss law.

Hunt returned to the Holy Land with his new bride and soon began work on the epic painting, *The Triumph of the Innocents*. A daughter, Gladys was born the following year and when the family returned to England they moved into Draycott Lodge in Fulham. This Regency house had been the home of Horace Walpole, and the Hunts soon decorated it with Morris wallpaper. A second son, Hilary arrived on the scene and although Hunt no longer displayed his work at the Royal Academy, he showed paintings at the Grosvenor and New Galleries.

For Hunt, the next few years would bring with them the deaths of many of his friends and associates including Rossetti, Morris, Madox Brown, Millais, Woolner and Burne-Jones. In 1902 the Hunt family needed to move from their comfortable home in Fulham and came to 18 Melbury Road, a sure sign of their artistic status. This was a prestigious address amidst The Holland Park Circle of artists that included William Burges and Lord Leighton. He continued to work, notably on his *Lady of Shalott* but from 1905 onwards he painted little.

He died on the 7th. September 1910 and he was interred in St. Paul's Cathedral by the side of Millais with the surviving William Rossetti amongst the pall bearers. Edith edited the second edition of her husband's memoirs as a tribute to his memory and lived until 1931when she was also buried in St. Paul's Cathedral.

John Everett Millais

FROM CHILD PRODIGY TO ESTABLISHMENT FIGURE

Although Millais was born in Southampton and therefore not that far from Sussex, his family of origin were prominent inhabitants of Jersey. He was born on the 8th. June 1829 and he spent many of his formative years on that island. Where it came to art he was very much a child prodigy and he was drawing extensively when he was only four years old. This ability did not help him at school where he never settled and from where he was expelled. Subsequently he received home tuition, partly due to his poor health at the time and also where he was more under the influence of his strong willed mother.

She and her husband took the young Millais to London in 1838 so that he might have the opportunity to develop his artistic talent. They met with the President of the Royal Academy who asked the boy to draw a piece of sculpture in front of him to prove that the impressive work, submitted in support of his application, was really his own. Whilst waiting for a place there, Millais enrolled at Sass's Art Academy where Rossetti would later claim to have been so bored! He also visited the National Gallery and British Museum, the latter being where he would first set eyes on Holman Hunt. Two years later he duly entered the Royal Academy at the incredible age of eleven and he was to spend the next six years there as a student.

During this time of much learning, he managed to keep in contact with two friends from his days in Jersey who were now at school in **Brighton.** It's doubtful however that he came down to the town as his friends, the Lempriere boys frequently visited London during their holidays. Arthur Lempriere would later be the model for the painting *The Huguenot.*

His first attempts at oil painting now appear rather stodgy (an example being the work in **Hove** museum) but it is in his drawings of the period that his precocious skills are more immediately obvious. Millais began to win awards much to the irritation of some of his fellow students (at Sass's, other students had hung Millais upside down from a window until he was unconscious because they were jealous of his talent) and he now worked in his studio at the family's home in Gower Street. This shows how his parents nurtured his talents and of all the principal Pre-Raphaelites, Millais had the least hardship and fewest obstacles in developing his early skill. Holman Hunt was glad of the chance to use Millais's studio facility from 1844 and it was not until 1848 that Rossetti came into their lives leading to the formation of the Brotherhood with Messrs Stephens, Woolner, Collinson and William Rossetti.

Millais's initial work in the new 'revolutionary' style was *Isabella* which had friends and family as models as well as the use of the mysterious PRB initials. Despite its radicalism it was well received by critics at the RA exhibition of 1849. The same could not be said the following year when his *Christ in the House of His Parents* was savaged by critics that included Charles Dickens. It was Millais's realistic depiction of the Holy Family as ordinary people with dirty finger nails and believable complexions that upset the correspondents of the time. Ruskin's impassioned defence of the movement a year later effectively put an end to this criticism but not before three further works by Millais had also been drubbed. These included *Mariana* and *The Woodman's Daughter* both worked on in Oxford. *Ophelia* followed, largely painted in Surrey and the source of one of the most famous Pre-Raphaelite tales ever (see chapter on Rossetti) involving the model for the work, Lizzie Siddal. It took Millais almost four months just to complete the figure of Ophelia, so meticulous was the detail.

In June 1852, Millais was once again tantalisingly close to Sussex when he took lodgings at Hayes, near Bromley in Kent. He was working on the background for *The Proscribed Royalist* which shows a Cavalier hiding from the Roundheads in an old oak tree. The tree was on a common nearby and for many years after was known as 'The Millais Oak' although now it can no longer be identified.

Millais finally set foot in Sussex when Hunt and Edward Lear were staying at **Fairlight** in July 1852. William Rossetti had just returned to London and when Millais arrived, the three went down to the beach below the impressive cliffs. Lear had been warned by Hunt that Millais was inclined to behave in a superior fashion and when the latter found some cuttlefish bones that he was interested in, he duly asked Lear to carry them for him. 'You carry it for me, King Lear' he said and Lear obliged, wherefore the expression 'He doesn't carry his own cuttlefish' became a memorable saying amongst the Brotherhood.

The next year, Millais asked Ruskin's wife Effie, to sit for him at his London studio. The work was to be called The *Order of Release* and for Effie the time away from her husband was indeed a 'release'. The friendship between Millais and the Ruskins increased and they then spent a working holiday together in Scotland, initially with Millais' brother William. As Millais drew and painted Effie amongst the wonderful landscape at Glenfinlas, romance blossomed. Effie began to confide in him about the unhappy state of her marriage. This had never been consummated and after Millais returned to London he wrote to her parents to express his concern for her well being. This provided the impetus for an eventual annulment of the marriage, but this did not occur until after prolonged legal wrangling and no little scandal. Because of this, Effie and Millais did not meet, so he once again threw himself into work.

He intended to paint two works, *The Blind Girl* and *L'Enfant du Regiment* (*The Random Shot*) and an unidentified friend suggested he might find appropriate backgrounds for both pictures at **Winchelsea.** Accompanied by Michael Halliday, another friend inspired by the works of the Brotherhood, he arrived in the area during the autumn of 1854. Whilst in the village, the two men occasionally partook of lunch at the New Inn. They were also joined by the novelist, William Thackeray who was writing *Denis Duval,* a novel left unfinished but whose central character is based on Millais.

Two tales survive from the time of Millais' visit to Winchelsea. The first concerns a local clergyman who repeatedly spoke to him of how inferior man's depiction of the world was in comparison to God's original. This diatribe took place in the church where Millais was working but despite the implied criticism, he steadfastly kept his cool and only broke into hysterical laughter after some time had elapsed. The second story is about another visitor to the church, a sexton who questioned Millais as to what he was doing in the building. Millais said words to the effect that he wished to paint the church, to which the sexton reassured Millais that he did not wish to waste his time and that the church was 'done up fresh last year'!

During the same period Halliday was painting his *Measuring for the Wedding Ring* which he exhibited at the Royal Academy two years later. Holman Hunt was in Jerusalem and he felt very homesick when he heard of the two painters being in Winchelsea, a town he had of course visited with Millais two years before.

1855 saw Millais and Effie's marriage and for a while they kept a reasonably low profile living at Bowerswell, near Perth in Scotland but also occasionally visiting

WINCHELSEA CHURCH - PHOTO BY AUTHOR

London. The wedding had caused a scandal and subsequently Queen Victoria would not receive Effie into her company until after Millais's death. *The Blind Girl* proved a success and was sold to the dealer, Gambart for 600 guineas although a number of critics disliked the work. *L'Enfant du Regiment* was exhibited at the Royal Academy where several senior members of the R A criticised both paintings leading to Millais feeling isolated and over sensitive. However, there was compensation in the birth of the couple's first son, Everett, the first of eight children.

The years 1857-9 saw Millais move away from the detailed, intricate work of his Pre-Raphaelite days to a broader, freer style. He continued to be out of favour with many colleagues and critics of the day, but developed his work in illustrating journals as well as a number of Trollope novels.

The Millais family was growing and in 1862 they moved into 7, Cromwell Place, Kensington although they continued to spend a part of every year in their beloved Scotland. Millais produced his first sentimentalised picture of a child (his daughter Effie, then aged five) perhaps because he was now in the bosom of his family. This work was *My First Sermon* (showing a child in a church pew actively listening) which was followed by *My Second Sermon* (same child asleep in the pew). It was thought that these two paintings may have been commenced whilst Millais was in the church at **Winchelsea** but the general opinion now is that they were painted in a church at Kingston-on Thames. The success of these two genre works led to Millais completing many more depictions of children, works both in subject and style far removed from his Pre-Raphaelite days.

The 1870's saw the first of his many large landscapes, the majority of which show Perthshire, the scenery that Millais found so inspirational. These are geographically and stylistically many miles away from his earlier work completed in Sussex. Although less detailed the later works are moodier and undeniably evocative of their subject.

Millais was by now a hugely successful artist and a member of the Victorian social elite, despite the early scandal of his marriage. He was now in demand as a portraitist and his many willing subjects included Lillie Langtry, Gladstone, Carlyle, Disraeli and Lord Tennyson. In 1878 he moved into the prestigious 2, Palace Gate in London and seven years later he was given a hereditary baronetcy. More fame followed with what is perhaps now regarded as Millais' artistic nadir. This took the form of *Bubbles*, a portrait of his grandson, William which became a ubiquitous sight when it was used for many years in an adapted form to advertise Pears soap.

As an establishment figure, Millais continued to paint for large commissions but was also influential in other artistic concerns such as the formation of the National Portrait Gallery in 1889. However his health began to decline from about 1892 following a serious bout of flu when he first noticed a swelling of his throat. This was to develop into cancer during the next four years. One more coveted appointment was to be his briefly before his death in 1896. Following the death of Lord Leighton he was elected President of the Royal Academy causing one commentator of the time to remark that he had 'gone a letter higher', he was PRA, whereas before he had been PRB.

Just before his death Queen Victoria finally relented and granted Effie an audience at court. Millais died aged 67 at his home and was buried at St Paul's cathedral on the 20th. August. In just over a year both his eldest son, Everett was also dead (of pneumonia) as was Effie who was buried in Perthshire, for so long the countryside loved by the two of them and their family.

Topsy and Ned

EDWARD BURNE-JONES AND WILLIAM MORRIS

Burne-Jones is a name synonymous with that of Pre-Raphaelitism although he produced his own unique interpretation of it and was a later exponent of the movement. In fact, Rossetti was something of a mentor and idol to the young Burne-Jones whose work bridges the gap between Pre-Raphaelite ideals and the beliefs underlining the later Aesthetic Movement, which in turn developed into art of a more abstract nature. His work also anticipated the emergence of Art Nouveau. Burne-Jones' name is also inseparable from that of William Morris although in terms of their connections to Sussex, it is Burne-Jones who has the stronger ties. (There is a separate section in this chapter that will look closely at the time he spent in Rottingdean where he leased a house from the early1880's).

Burne-Jones' life had its beginnings in an altogether different environment- that of heavily industrialised Birmingham, with its accompanying poverty and hardship. Ted Jones (as he was until he decided he did not wish to be just one of the Jones') was born on the 28th. August 1833 and from the outset his life was tinged with sadness. As a result of the birth his mother died within a week and his father reacted badly to this. They had already suffered the grief of losing their first child Edith and the young Burne-Jones was cared for by a succession of nanny figures until the arrival of a Miss Sampson, who was to be a secure if conservative presence in his early life. His father was a quiet man who made a barely adequate living as a framer and gilder although they did reside in a comparatively respectable part of the city. The isolation that Burne-Jones experienced meant that he spent much of his time alone, drawing or reading books such as *Aesop's Fables*. It may also account for the lifelong dislike of his contemporary world and subsequent withdrawal into another world of his own making.

In 1844 at the age of eleven he started attending the local King Edward School where he was to flourish although life there could be tough. On one occasion, he was stabbed during morning prayers, but he did establish some important friendships, including that of the future educationalist Cormell (Crom) Price, who would prove to be a lifelong ally. It was also during this time that he became interested in the High Church (Oxford) Movement that was then very active with leaders such as Cardinal Newman. Visits to places such as Hereford Cathedral increased his interest in the church and so he decided to follow this vocational path rather than become an engineer (an idea of his fathers). No doubt it was the spectacle and mystique of the religious ceremonies that attracted Burne-Jones but it was an idea that persisted and was to lead on to other career choices. In 1853, a year before he attended Exeter College at Oxford he was introduced to his future wife Georgiana by her brother Harry MacDonald, a school friend of Burne-Jones. She would become his biographer and loyal support through his frequent periods of ill health. In another family connection, Georgiana's elder sister Alice would later marry Rudyard Kipling's father so that Burne-Jones would become his uncle.

It was at Oxford that he met William Morris, a man from a far more affluent background, but there was an immediate bond between the two men. They and their friends began to read medieval romances and other contemporary authors such as

Edgar Allan Poe and Tennyson amongst others. They were also both in agreement with their dislike of all things ugly, a condition that Morris was later to ascribe to the inhabitants of Brighton! They decided to produce a magazine in order to spread their beliefs and ideas about how the society of the time was losing its way with rampant industrialisation, materialism and moral decline. They felt much could be learnt from the past. *The Oxford and Cambridge Magazine,* as it was called, contained Morris's verse as well as other poetry, essays and literary criticism. It was a relatively short term venture but helped to clarify the groups concerns and certainly encouraged conversation in a similar way that the earlier *The Germ* had done for the first wave of Pre-Raphaelites.

The two friends decided to tour the churches and cathedrals of France and not surprisingly these proved to be an inspiration and a confirmation of their ideas. They could not help but admire the craftsmanship and skill of the medieval worker. It was after this trip that they stood on the port at Le Havre and decided their future paths. Morris was to be an architect and Burne-Jones, despite a lack of experience and training, was to become a painter.

Returning home, they both became increasingly aware of people like Rossetti and Holman Hunt, partly through seeing their works but also via the writings and teachings of Ruskin. The still unbearded Burne-Jones then set about making the acquaintance of Rossetti whose work he particularly admired and when this was duly arranged, Rossetti announced that he had met 'the nicest fellow in dreamland'. Burne-Jones left Oxford without obtaining a degree and Rossetti was to be instrumental in helping Burne-Jones get his first artistic commissions on his arrival in London.

Whilst Burne-Jones was meeting a number of people friendly with Rossetti, Morris successfully passed his degree and started work in the offices of G.E. Street, the influential architect. There he met Philip Webb and another important partnership began to prosper. When Street's office moved to London, Morris and Burne-Jones were reunited and they took an apartment together. This helped create the right milieu for collaborative working and would later culminate in the formation of a company for the promotion of the decorative arts.

The influence of that much read book *Morte D'Arthur* was never far away and in 1857 an opportunity arrived through Rossetti to decorate the debating room at the Oxford Union with mural scenes from those tales of King Arthur. These were not a complete success but did bring people together as well as being the time that Morris first encountered Jane Burden, later to become Mrs. Morris. Also under Rossetti's intense enthusiasm Morris gave up wishing to be an architect in order to concentrate on design. Rossetti was also responsible for suggesting Burne-Jones designed stained glass for Powell and Sons and this was to be his first foray into this area. The glass was for a church at Maidstone in Kent and led onto further work for another glass firm, Lavers and Barraud. Now Burne-Jones grew his beard for the first time and that distinctive profile was born.

The years of 1859/60 were marked by three weddings- Morris and Jane, Rossetti and Lizzie Siddall, and after a lengthy engagement, Burne-Jones and Georgiana MacDonald. It was rather predictable that a planned joint honeymoon in Paris for the latter two couples should not happen due to another bout of illness suffered by Burne-Jones. 1860 was also the year that Morris set out to design and build a dream house for his new wife and friends when he acquired some land at Bexleyheath in Kent for this purpose. He wisely left the architectural side of things to Webb whilst everyone else got involved in the other aspects of decoration and design. The Red House is now seen

ST. MICHAEL AND ALL ANGELS CHURCH IN BRIGHTON - PHOTO BY AUTHOR

as a forerunner of modern architecture and all the joint working involved led to the formation of Morris, Marshall Faulkner and Co. The company members included Burne-Jones, Webb, Rossetti and Madox Brown as well as a surveyor, P.P. Marshall, and Charles Faulkner who was a mathematician. The last two partner's names were used in addition to that of Morris for the title, as it was felt this would emphasise a sensible side to the endeavour rather than an artistic prevalence.

In the same year, Burne-Jones was asked by the architect George Frederick Bodley, who was friendly with the group, to paint an altarpiece for **St. Paul's Church** in **Brighton.** Bodley was not the architect of the church (that was Richard Cromwell Carpenter) but had been called in to suggest a focus for the church interior. His idea led to the largest painting to date by Burne-Jones, but when it was completed he felt it appeared unclear from a distance and therefore set about painting a second version. In this he got rid of the shepherds from an *Adoration* scene and this version of the altarpiece remained in the church until 1975. It was then loaned to Brighton Museum for a while before being bought at auction by Andrew Lloyd-Webber. The first version came back into Bodley's hands and is now in the collection of the Tate Gallery.

The company's breakthrough to commercial success was provided by an appearance at the International Exhibition at what is now the Victoria and Albert Museum in 1862. Here, seven stained glass panels by Rossetti called *The Parable of the Vineyard*, aroused much interest (some people actually believed them to be medieval) and several commissions followed. Burne-Jones wrote to Crom who was now tutoring in Russia to tell him of their accomplishments. One of the commissions was again from Bodley (an important connection forged by Morris in earlier times) and was to supply fittings to a new church he was building in **Brighton - St. Michael and All Angels,**

Bodley's work was influenced by both Ruskin and Street and his church was to be in French/Italian Gothic style. Morris, Webb and Faulkner decorated the roof of the chancel with their own hands which took them about five days. Madox Brown, Burne-Jones and Marshall in addition were involved in the designs for the stained glass. The rival firm of Clayton and Bell had already begun work on glazing some of the windows but this did not deter Morris and the others from completing some of their most inspired early work. It proved to be a family affair with other female family members assisting with the making of cloths and vestments and in the painting of tiles.

In the next few years Burne-Jones' style evolved and he was increasingly influenced by the Italian painters of The Renaissance. He had visited Italy twice in 1859 and 1861and would later go again this time in the company of Ruskin. He was now a father (Philip, his son was born in October 1861 and went on to become a reasonably successful portrait painter) and it was important to have regular forms of income. Exhibiting with the Old Water-Colour Society helped his financial situation and also led to him meeting such fellow artists as Henry Holiday and Albert Moore being already conversant with William De Morgan and Spencer Stanhope.

Burne-Jones' more assured financial position meant that in 1867 he and his growing family (his daughter Margaret arrived in June 1866) could move into a larger property, The Grange in Fulham which at the time was in an almost rural area. This was only possible because of his popularity with members of the new wealthy middle class who became his patrons. His fame spread and despite setbacks (he had to withdraw a picture from view on one occasion because of an outcry over its nudity) his star was definitely on the ascendant. However there was to be much greater conflict in his life due to the appearance of a Maria Zambaco.

Burne-Jones met her through his contact with the Ionides family who were rich patrons of the arts. She was separated from her husband who was living in Paris with their two children and was a practising artist. Maria was very much a 'stunner' in the true Pre-Raphaelite sense and she began to model for Burne-Jones on a regular basis. There are many beautiful, intimate drawings of her which suggest that his feelings for her were very deep. An affair ensued and dragged on, reaching its zenith in 1871 when Maria threatened suicide and Burne-Jones' marriage to Georgiana nearly broke down under the strain. He had many bouts of depression in the years that followed, no doubt some as a result of the doomed affair.

But his art continued to rise in popularity. He was able to employ studio assistants in the form of Thomas Rooke and Charles Fairfax-Murray. His paintings was more in the vein of the High Renaissance and he was the sole designer for a revamped Morris and Co. In 1877 he started to exhibit at the newly opened Grosvenor gallery and this included such works as *The Beguiling of Merlin* and *The Mirror of Venus*. It was here that he met many leading socialites of the day including Ellen Terry, Oscar Wilde and Aubrey Beardsley.

Burne-Jones was rapidly becoming a famous figure and typically he sought some respite from all the attention, and so it was in late 1877 that he took a trip to the seaside.

ROTTINGDEAN

Burne-Jones' success meant that he could now afford to buy a country retreat. Georgiana could see what positive benefits the air outside of London might have on her husband's health and well being. But he was in a quandary about where the best place to escape might be. He wrote 'I should like the sea, but I hate Brighton, and I love Oxford, but it isn't the sea'. He decided to go to Brighton for a few days and whilst there walked out along the cliffs eventually coming into Rottingdean, then a smaller and quieter village than it is today. He did a drawing of the church and then sketched some characters he described as coastguards who he noted 'peer through telescopes suddenly, as if the Armada was in sight and they must give the alarm'.

This trip was also noteworthy because of the purchase of two owls at a bazaar on the old Chain Pier. Burne-Jones bought these with his friend Eustace Balfour (an architect who was twenty one years his junior and a future Prime Minister) and the birds were duly named Socrates and Eustacia. They were brought back to London where their eating habits left much to be desired resulting in their departure to a friend of Mr. Balfour's who lived in Cambridgeshire. Not all was over however, and about a year later Burne-Jones wrote from Paris to tell Georgiana that another owl was on its way. This is fairly typical of his humour in that on arrival the bird proved to be a plaster cast!

The decision was made that Rottingdean would make an ideal location for a second home and this became even more of a priority following the stresses involved in the Whistler vs. Ruskin libel case, where Burne-Jones was a witness for Ruskin. In 1880, Georgiana was down in Sussex scouring the area for an appropriate house. Having had no luck in Brighton she then walked in a roundabout way to Rottingdean arriving from the north. She saw Prospect House standing empty by the green and bought it at once.

W.A.S. Benson was asked to help improve the house and this he did both architecturally and in terms of interior design. A few months later the Burne-Jones family were finally able to move into their new home.

CLOSE UP OF AUBREY COTTAGE SHOWING SOME OF W.A.S. BENSONS ALTERATIONS - PHOTO BY AUTHOR

Almost immediately the relaxing atmosphere of the house and the surrounding landscape influenced Burne-Jones' output. He commenced his series of water-colours that would make up his *Flower Book*. These surprisingly were not individual flower studies but a series of poetically titled illustrations sometimes in the name of flowers. An example of one of the roundels is called *Rose of Heaven* and this shows a sea nymph figure being transported by birds from the sea towards the sky. This type of subject was a popular one of the time when Burne-Jones was fascinated by the sea and its mermaids and mermen, no doubt as a result of his new surroundings.

In 1882 there were several holidays at Rottingdean with Morris and Jane coming down as well as old friends like Crom who was now Rudyard Kipling's headmaster. Morris came down with his eldest daughter and they visited the aquarium at Brighton- '*I think I saw more ugly people in Brighton than I have seen otherwise for the last twenty years*' and Lewes- '*on the whole it is set down better than any town I have seen in England, unluckily it is not a very interesting town in itself*'. He also considered all the churches to have been badly restored, a frequent concern of his in this time of mass 'restoration'. Morris found the house '*very pleasant and agreeable and suits me to a T*'.

Thomas Rooke was also present (he however slept in the village) helping Burne-Jones in the converted studio that looked over to the church. They both loved this view and it would provide an occasional distraction from the work in preparation. This included *Arthur in Avalon* which was to be his great unfinished masterpiece (it now resides in Puerto Rico, a sign of how unpopular the work of Burne-Jones was at the time of its sale).

The following January brought forth a tirade from the artist when he wrote that he hated winter with '*its rain, wind, cold, sleet, frost, fog, iced baths, snow, slush, mud,...*' etc. He always wanted Rottingdean to be restorative and when it wasn't (normally due to the weather) he was disappointed. Later, in May 1891 a visit there did not prevent him catching influenza on his return to Fulham, a condition that always dragged him down for long periods. Similarly in 1893, the refreshing winds gave him toothache, an unexpected problem.

But back in 1883 Burne-Jones was attempting to come to terms with Rossetti's death (they had seen less of one another for a number of years) and with regard to this he was grateful for the peace and quiet offered by '*a little village near hateful Brighton*'.

Two years later he was offered an associate-ship of the Royal Academy and the only work he ever submitted there was a painting inspired and completed at Rottingdean. Called *The Depths of the Sea* it depicts a mermaid dragging a dead sailor to the bottom of the ocean. It is rather sinister and menacing and caused a bit of a stir when exhibited. The interest in these ladies of the deep led later to a room in Prospect House being called the Merry Mermaid and being decorated in the manner of a tavern. The same year he designed four stained glass windows for an upstairs landing of the house. Supplied by Morris & Co. their subject was from the beloved *Morte d'Arthur*, a subject Burne-Jones had not used for some fifteen years. Such figures as Sir Lancelot, Sir Gawaine and Sir Galahad are depicted in their search for the Holy Grail. In a way they can be seen as prototypes for the famous large scale Holy Grail tapestries that Morris and Burne-Jones would collaborate on a few years later. These wonderful panels are no longer in situ but are in the possession of the Victoria and Albert Museum.

Morris visited Rottingdean in February 1887 for what sounds like a busman's holiday-he was in the process of translating *The Odyssey!*

Later that year a seemingly happy family event occurred when Margaret, Burne-Jones' daughter became engaged to John W. Mackail (the future biographer of Morris)

THE WINDOW OF ST. MARGARET AT ROTTINGDEAN - PHOTO BY AUTHOR

and the couple planned to marry in the village church at Rottingdean. The thought of 'losing' his daughter appears to have rather unnerved Burne-Jones, who thought that his future son-in-law had got to know Margaret by ostensibly discussing literature with him. He wrote '*Here is my darling Margaret on whom I depend for everything and without whom I should crumble into senility in an hour - and what has she done? Yes, what indeed, but engaged herself.*'

He continued to be agitated until the day of the wedding which was the 4th. September 1888, when he seems to have relaxed accepting positively the inevitable. He wrote '*Margaret walked between Georgie and me and it seemed to rain rose-leaves-that was the only rain there was, for the sky was bright windy blue.*' A happy father agreed to make a three light window to commemorate the wedding and Burne-Jones himself visited the church in 1893 to see the workmen put the last window in.

A year after the marriage Burne-Jones was able to purchase the adjacent property (Aubrey Cottage) and Benson was asked to oversee the alterations. There was now more room for the family and friends and another studio area was created as well as a new entrance to the building. He wrote to his confidante Frances Horner about how enjoyable his birthday was that year with one of his presents being a map '*that has big sea monsters ramping and foaming off Rottingdean, and the battle of Hastings in one corner, and the French fleet in Pevensey Bay, and Hurstmonceux is there*'.

This was a time of frequent travel between Fulham and Rottingdean. But these were to be the last years of Burne-Jones' life and Morris was already not so well. Their last great collaborative effort was to be with printing and the formation of the Kelmscott Press with their book of Chaucer in particular. Many of its 87 illustrations were done at Rottingdean and it is fair to say that the sheer quality of the reproduction of this book is unlikely to ever be surpassed.

Gladstone gave Burne-Jones a baronetcy in 1894 as an acknowledgement of his work and he reluctantly accepted this.

On the local scene, in 1896 he told Rooke, his studio assistant, how pleased he was when a gale brought down the Brighton to Rottingdean electric railway. This vehicle was known locally as 'daddy-longlegs' and was obviously a symbol to Burne-Jones of how the world was going the wrong way, with even this bizarre form of transport leading to easier travel between the village and Brighton, an undesirable development. As it was he already found Rottingdean to be '*full of donkeys and babies*', and comments such as these meant that he was not always popular with other residents.

Morris died the same year and it must have been an enormous blow. In his last few years Burne-Jones retreated into himself even more and devoted a lot more time to the monumental *Arthur in Avalon*. After a whole days work on this canvas on the 16th. June 1898 Burne-Jones and Georgiana had a pleasant evening with visitors and after reading

OLD POSTCARD SHOWING 'DADDY LONG LEGS' - PHOTO COURTESY OF STEVE BENZ

and writing a letter to his nephew, Rudyard Kipling he retired to bed. Early the next morning Burne-Jones suffered a heart attack and died.

Three days later his ashes were interred in a corner of the church wall in a spot that is now marked and visible from the house. It was a place he had chosen and discussed with Georgie years before. An account at the time described the events: '(there was) a mellow light cast by windows in the quiet country church at Rottingdean on the afternoon of June 21st. 1898. The funeral service of the great artist was conducted and in the sunny south-west angle just without, his ashes repose, ringed around by flowering red and white valerium'.

On the 23rd. June there was a memorial service at Westminster Abbey, the first one to take place there in order to honour an artist.

Georgiana continued to live in the village for another 22 years during which time she caused a few ripples. On one occasion, she draped a pro-Boer banner on the outside of the house and the police needed to be present as an angry crowd gathered. She was also supportive of the suffragette movement. She died in 1920 and was then reunited with her husband in the grounds of the church.

THE GRAVE STONES OF BURNE - JONES AND GEORGIANA EMBEDDED IN THE WALL OF THE CHURCH WITH ANGELA THIRKELL'S WOODEN GRAVE MARKER IN THE FOREGROUND - PHOTO BY AUTHOR

Minor Artists

AND LOCAL RESPONSES TO THE PRE-RAPHAELITES

TWO LOCAL ARTISTS

CHARLES EAMER KEMPE (1837-1907)

C. E. Kempe was by any standard, one of the most prolific and successful of all Victorian stained glass makers. However, the immense popularity that he enjoyed at the time has now largely disappeared, but despite this his work is to be seen everywhere. There is almost no part of the country where you are further than 30 miles from a church containing some of his stained glass or other ecclesiastical furniture such as a reredos, altar or screen.

He was born on the 29th. June 1837 at Ovingdean Hall near **Brighton,** the son of Nathaniel Kemp, whose uncle was Thomas Read Kemp, the founder of Kemp Town in Brighton. The different spelling of his surname is simply because he preferred the additional 'e'. The location of his birthplace means that much of his early work is fortuitously to be found in this county.

A WINDOW BY C.E. KEMPE IN OVINGDEAN CHURCH - PHOTO BY AUTHOR

Educated at Pembroke College, Oxford he intended to take up Holy Orders but like Burne-Jones changed his mind. Kempe's decision was largely based on a realisation that his speech impediment would interfere with the need to spread God's word.

He decided to study architecture (like Morris) and became the pupil of George Frederick Bodley. He soon realised that his main interest lay in the design of stained glass and spent some time in the workshops of the firm, Clayton & Bell. In 1862, he designed the lectern for the church of **St Michael and All Angels** in **Brighton** at the same time as Morris was undertaking an important early commission. By the mid-1860's he was designing independently and in 1869 undertook the decoration of the ceiling at the **Holy Trinity church** in **Cuckfield** as well as designing the lychgate. Continuing to work in London he moved into a house called Old Place in **Lindfield** where he held services in his private oratory.

Kempe's early designs were his strongest, although ironically it is these which sometimes go unnoticed as they lack a clear means of identification. His use of mainly blue, green and ruby colours with the detail apparent in his figure painting leads to comparisons being made to work by established followers of Pre-Raphaelitism. It is doubtful however whether he had more than the briefest contacts with people like Morris or Burne-Jones although in the 1860's Kempe almost went into partnership with another Pre-Raphaelite Arthur Hughes.

From 1895 Kempe used the familiar wheatsheaf motif (adapted from the family arms) to identify his work. For much of the time his work retained its individuality and quality although there are criticisms that his glass designs were becoming a little repetitive.

He died unexpectedly on the 29th.April 1907 and was buried at **Ovingdean** in the family tomb beside the church that he had helped restore in the earlier days of his career. His studios continued to operate with Kempe's nephew, Walter Tower as the Chairman, until 1934 when they finally closed. The work completed after Kempe's death does often pale in comparison with the early work but can still be pleasing. There is a good deal of it in Sussex, identified as it is by the wheatsheaf symbol with an additional tower emblem emblazoned over it.

The gazetteer has details of many Kempe windows and other designs but the essential ones to visit are at: Brighton (the Churches of St. Augustine and St. Peter), Cuckfield, Danehill, Fletching, Lavant, Lindfield, Ovingdean, Partridge Green, Staplefield, Turners Hill, Worthing (St. Andrew)

HARRY MILEHAM (1873-1957)

Although born as late as 1873, Harry Mileham was a Pre-Raphaelite at the same time as followers such as John Byam Shaw and Eleanor Fortescue Brickdale. He also lived much of his life in **Brighton and Hove** where he has left examples of his work and where he was President for many years of the Brighton Arts Club.

Coming from an old Norfolk family, he was educated in London before joining the Royal Academy in 1892. There, he attended classes overseen by such luminary teachers as Leighton, Dicksee, Alma-Tadema and Poynter. The students alongside him included Byam Shaw as well as Arthur Rackham. A little later, Mileham's cousin Gilbert Holiday attended the R.A. who was a relative of Henry Holiday.

Mileham travelled widely and particularly liked Italy where he developed a keenness for painting biblical scenes. He was also being influenced by the work of the Pre-Raphaelites, whose work he would have seen in a number of memorial exhibitions, as this was the time that many of the original advocates of the movement were coming to the end of their lives. There was also more of their work on display in galleries as well as being more accessible through reproduction. Mileham liked the national nature of their work and saw himself as an English artist when France and Paris in particular, were so influential.

He generally preferred the early work of Holman Hunt and Madox Brown to the more Italianate styled Burne-Jones and Rossetti. In fact one of his works, *Alfred presents a royal cloak and sword to his grandson Athelstan* of 1909 even has **Sompting** Church in its background in an undeniable homage to Madox Brown's *Wycliffe Reading his Translation of the New Testament to his Protector, John of Gaunt.*

In 1916, Mileham, his wife and two sons moved to **Brighton.** They were all distressed by the recent death of the eldest daughter, Faith from a viral infection. The boys attended Prestonville Preparatory School and later, Brighton College. Mileham became involved in staging costumed pageants which made him a comparatively well known figure locally. But it was in the twenties and thirties that he achieved real prominence as a church decorator. This included the design of stained glass windows and altarpieces. His style continued to gain clear inspiration from other artists but was

A DETAIL SHOWING HARRY MILEHAM'S MONOGRAM FROM A STAINED GLASS WINDOW IN ST STEPHENS CHURCH BEXHILL - PHOTO BY AUTHOR

also developing into a unique form. Influences as diverse as Botticelli, Watts and increasingly Burne-Jones are evident in his finished work. Mileham successfully completed decorative schemes for a number of churches in the **Brighton** area as well as in other parts of Sussex.

His wife, Kathleen became increasingly unwell throughout the thirties and died shortly after a move to a house called 'Burlingham' in Mallory Road, in 1938. This was obviously a major setback for Mileham but he later remarried, and continued to work until his death in 1957.

Examples of his work can be found at Church of The Good Shepherd, Brighton, St. Stephen's Church, Bexhill

OTHER ARTISTS

ALBERT GOODWIN (1845-1932)

Goodwin was born in Maidstone, Kent and after his schooling was apprenticed to a draper in the town. He was lucky enough to have his talent for art noticed by a local printer who happened to know Holman Hunt. The story goes that Hunt in turn introduced the young Goodwin to Arthur Hughes and the two were destined to have a lifelong friendship. Hughes convinced Goodwin's parents to let their son (he was only in his early teens) be tutored by him. This later led to Goodwin becoming a pupil of Madox Brown and an acquaintance with Rossetti, William Bell Scott, Morris and others. He also came to know John Ruskin who became a considerable influence on the young artist, the two men later touring Europe together.

Goodwin was essentially a landscape artists and his early intense and atmospheric work drew heavily on the inspiration of the members of the then disbanded Brotherhood. He was a very prolific painter whose subject matter changed little although like many of his contemporaries his later style became broader but compositionally more interesting.

In 1867 he moved to **Arundel** where he was married although his wife was to die two years later. He also lived for a short time at Waterloo Street in **Hove**. After remarrying and periods of living in London and Devon he moved back into Sussex in 1906 at **Bexhill**. He spent the years until his death in 1932 at a house called Ellerslie at Highwoods near the seaside town.

His works include many moody depictions of local scenes which show a particular interest in the effects of light and sun and sudden weather changes. There are examples of his work in all the major municipal galleries in the county with Hastings having a particularly large and impressive collection.

GEORGE PRICE BOYCE (1826-1897)

Boyce is perhaps best known now as a chronicler of the Pre-Raphaelites (in his Diaries) and also as an important collector of their works. However, he was also a talented painter, working mainly in watercolour with primarily landscape subjects. His early influences included the artist David Cox and it was through his acquaintance with Thomas Seddon that he met Rossetti around 1850 with whom he would remain a lifelong friend.

At this time he found himself laid up at **Hastings** where he painted a detailed study of *The Castle Rock* from his bedroom window. He was developing a Pre-Raphaelite style which he would continue to use for a number of years.

In 1853 he got to know Millais and Hunt. He was friendly with Millais from the start but like others at the time found Hunt difficult. He was also encouraged in his work by Ruskin and subsequently visited Venice. He travelled widely throughout his life also going to Egypt in the footsteps of both Seddon and Holman Hunt.

'CASTLE ROCK' BY GEORGE PRICE BOYCE - PERMISSION OF WILLIAMSON ART GALLERY BIRKENHEAD

Nearer to home, in 1857 he was in Sussex at **Haywards Heath** and **Petworth** where he probably painted his *Girl by a Beech Tree* in a landscape that is now in the collection of Tate Britain.

Boyce continued to paint until the early 1890's and gradually developed a looser style with a more restrained range of tones and colours. He worked alongside Philip Webb in the Society for the Preservation of Ancient Buildings and also had a house built by him in Chelsea where Boyce died in February 1897.

WALTER CRANE(1845-1915)

Crane is best known today as an illustrator of children's books. He also completed a comparatively small amount of paintings which in the main, owe much to the style of Burne-Jones.

Early on in his career he was apprenticed to a wood engraver and in the 1860's began working in black and white illustration influenced by the work of Millais and Rossetti. Around this time he visited Sussex in the company of an uncle and spent a fortnight sketching and drawing. This was in the **Arundel** and **Littlehampton** area and Crane wrote about how much he enjoyed picnicking in the garden of the Black Rabbit pub (still there today).

At the beginning of the next decade his illustrated books were in wide circulation and his fame led him into the circles of Morris, Burne-Jones, Philip Webb and William DeMorgan. He was also in love and due to be married, and spent time with his bride to be at **Fairlight Glen,** a location he knew through Holman Hunt's earlier picture (*Our English Coasts*).

In 1882 after more success in china design and wallpapers and now with a family, he returned to **Littlehampton** which he still liked. The family were visited by Edward Robert Hughes, the painter and nephew of Arthur Hughes. He completed a portrait of Crane's two sons.

He returned to Sussex for brief periods of time in 1890 (**Winchelsea**, a water-colour of the church is in the collection at Worthing) and 1893 (**Bosham**). In these later years he became close to the Socialist movement like his friend, William Morris. His influence on the Art and Crafts Movement in both Europe and America continued to be strong until the end of the century. He died in London in 1915.

Standen

Standen lies in beautiful, delectable landscape a little to the south of East Grinstead, overlooking the Medway valley. The site was found in 1890 for James Beale, a successful London solicitor, who lived with his wife Margaret and their seven children in fashionable Holland Park, London. He wanted to create a house that was not grand, but informal and would function as both a weekend retreat and holiday home as well as ultimately, a place to spend retirement. Beale was a self made man and certainly not a member of the landed gentry, then so well known for their lavish parties. His desire was to put some distance between his family and the outside world and it was through friends that he heard of an architect appropriate for the job in hand.

That man was Philip Webb and Beale asked him to design the house. Webb was of course a lifelong friend of William Morris having initially met him when they worked together in the offices of G.E.Street, the architect. In 1860, he had completed the famous Red House in Bexleyheath, Kent for Morris's personal use.

When Webb came to view the Standen site in 1891 to become familiar with the district, there was already a man named Simpson at work on the garden. Typically two of Webb's early decisions were to suggest a change of aspect for the house and to disagree with Simpson on the style of garden most suitable. Ironically, much of the garden's subsequent development was not due to either men, but as a result of Mrs.

STANDEN EAST GRINSTEAD - BY KIND PERMISSION OF THE NATIONAL TRUST

Margaret Beale's enthusiasm.

A number of plans for the house were subsequently drawn up, which initially proved to be too extravagant for the Beales's finances and features such as a library, disappeared with revisions. Eventually a plan was agreed between the parties which also kept some of the existing vernacular buildings at the location including a fifteenth century farmhouse. Webb had an appreciation of the traditions of English domestic architecture and incorporated older buildings and other historical elements into his plans. Client and architect generally got on well despite Webb's fiery reputation and socialist principles. The house was to be a home to live in rather than a building to be admired.

Between 1892-4 the house was constructed at a cost of about £18000 by the local builder, Peter Peters of Horsham to Webb's designs. In tandem with his belief that older buildings should be incorporated into new developments, Webb was also an innovator in his use of new science, an example being the early use of electricity in the house. There was also central heating from the outset.

His designs proved successful and over the years there were few changes to the house as it ran smoothly for its inhabitants and was comfortable if idiosyncratic. However another local building firm, Charles Rice of East Grinstead, did execute some later changes, all to Webb's specifications. These included a pair of workman's cottages in 1896, and two years later the installation of a bay window to the hall and a recess to the billiard room.

Webb believed that the entrance to a house should be mysterious and encourage expectation from the visitor. This was achieved by not having all the house in view at any one time. There is no sudden vista of the house instead it slowly reveals its charms. A modest lane overhung with rock outcrops (a former quarry) opens out onto what appears to be a village green. Bounded on three sides by buildings, it is here we find

GOOSE GREEN AT STANDEN - BY KIND PERMISSION OF THE NATIONAL TRUST

the old Sussex farmhouse with its Horsham tiled roof. The entrance to the house is then found through an arch that connects the farmhouse to a low level service wing. It is not until you are in the garden and the south front is visible that you begin to see the house as a unified whole. There is a tapestry of building materials evident which because of the exposed position of the house even includes pebbledash! In addition, there is local stone quarried on site, Horsham brick, tiling and weatherboarding as well as a mix of Georgian sash windows and leaded casement windows.

The interior has a host of features designed by Webb and these range from the small to the grand. All the fireplaces were designed by him and no two are the same. Even the brass fingerplates on the doors were Webb's invention. Standen was a late Morris & Co. project and it is therefore unlikely that Morris was personally involved although Webb himself chose many of the original furnishings, furniture and paintings. The great irony in view of both men's socialist leanings is that only wealthy clients such as the Beales could afford many of the Company's furnishings particularly as they were made in a superior way to take account of an individual tradesman's skills.

The Beales were happy with their new home and it was to be a focus of family life for over seventy years. For the first twenty years or so it was used in addition to their London home. James Beale was a regular golf player at the nearby Ashdown Forest club and encouraged his sons to become proficient in shooting. When he died in 1912, Margaret, his widow continued to live at Standen until her death in 1936. Some of the 'children' got married and set up their own homes, coming down to visit for holidays and special occasions. Maggie, the second eldest lived at Standen after her mother and then in 1947 the house passed to the youngest daughter, Helen. It was she who bequeathed it to the National Trust in 1972 thereby guaranteeing its survival as almost the only Webb house left unscathed by later development.

There is a fine account of life at Standen in the excellent guidebook available and space prevents me from describing this or the present contents of the house in too much detail. However I will add a few amusing and interesting anecdotes from the house's past as well as highlighting a few items of note in the rooms. To the author's embarrassment there was once a butler by the name of Wise who was found to be worse for the effects of drink and subsequently dismissed!

When you tour the house you may wish to look out for the following items of interest in addition to using the guidebook notes.

Upon entering the Porch (where the Aunt Beales' would have gathered to greet the arrival of their nieces and nephews in early motor cars) take a look at the bronze relief immediately in front of you. This is entitled *The Vision*, dates from 1893 and is by George Frampton. Frampton was a sculptor who was particularly inspired by Burne-Jones whose work he had discovered in Paris in 1889. He was one of a small number of artists who brought a three dimensional component to Pre-Raphaelite art.

In the Hall are examples of Mrs. Beale's embroidery skills as well as some of the glass lampshades made by Powells to a design by W.A.S. Benson. These appear throughout the house and are a stylish example of Benson's work, a man who would later become the chairman of Morris & Co.

In the Billiard Room, look out for the four small but exquisite drawings by Henry Stacy Marks, a figure on the peripheries of the Pre-Raphaelites. Although not original to the house, it is appropriate that they are here as Marks wrote extensively about individuals such as Ruskin and Millais and deserves to be more widely known. It was also here that Helen Beale would sometimes show the men how to play billiards properly! George Jack did the panelling and bookshelves in 1907, a man whom it seems regularly had to remind Webb that he owed him money.

In the Conservatory Corridor is an example of the first Morris produced pattern for wallpaper, made in 1862. Called 'Trellis' the birds shown on it had to be completed by Webb as Morris had difficulty drawing them. When it first appeared it was thought to be old fashioned and this was probably because of its naturalistic representation. At the time other Victorian patterns and designs were far more stylised. Also here, is a set of scales that were used to weigh the various children on arrival and departure and to settle bets as to which one had put the most weight on in just one meal!

Passing through the heated conservatory we arrive in the Drawing Room. This sumptuous room has examples of art and design by many of the principal figures associated with the Pre-Raphaelites. The wall lights are by Webb with the standard and table lights designed by Benson. The wallpaper is another Morris creation and there is further furniture by George Jack. Of note is his Saville armchair with its arm supports and legs in the shape of balusters, completed in Utrecht Velvet. There is another similar chair in the Hall and the curvy outline of the struts under the arm are thought to be characteristic of Jack's work. There is in addition a painting by Edward Stott (see Trail No. 14) in this room. Curiously, there is also a small plaster relief by that other connection to Amberley, Robert Anning Bell, in the Westbourne Bedroom. Before reaching the bedrooms there is another example of Frampton's output in the large plaster relief of *Mary and Agnes*. This is to be seen hanging on the opposite wall to Madox Brown's *The Baptism of King Edwin* on the Staircase.

The bedrooms on the first floor give a good impression of how radically light and uncluttered Morris and Webb's interiors were in comparison with many of the late Victorian era. They also provide a contrast to the dark richness of the interiors at Red House. It was in these rooms that generations of Beale children slept after 'promotion' from the nursery. They sometimes complained that the large amount of cupboards and drawers meant that they were inclined to lose their belongings!

In the North Bedroom are the hangings embroidered in silk by Mrs. Beale and her daughters, Amy, Maggie and Dorothy. Based on Morris's *Artichoke* design it shows the influence of Near Eastern and Italian weaves on Morris in the 1870's. There is also a charming pastel by Burne-Jones. This is dated 1885, the year that Burne-Jones was elected an Associate of the Royal Academy from which eight years later he resigned. The adjacent Dressing Room has an impressive selection of Pre-Raphaelite work with chalks, watercolours and drawings by the likes of Rossetti, George Howard, Sandys, Rooke and Henry Holiday.

Downstairs again, there is the Dining Room with its attractive blue-green decoration which was very popular in the 1890's when it was called 'William and Mary'. The stainless steel cheeks within the fireplace came from a design that Webb originally produced for the gallery fireplace at Constantine Ionides house in Hove (see Trail No1). The final principal room is the Morning Room, the domain primarily of the ladies of the house. Here again are examples of furniture whose origins go back to the medieval influences so important to the Pre-Raphaelites. A good illustration of this is the seven legged circular table designed by Webb and original to the house. This would have come from Morris's standard range and was designed from the 1860's. There is other furniture that is more refined in style and encapsulates influences such as oriental sources. Also in this room is a table lamp by Benson, made of brass and copper and probably supplied through the Morris & Co. shop. Benson set up his own workshop for turned metalwork in the 1880's.

You leave the house via the Service Wing passing what was once the Butler's Pantry and the Servant's Hall heading towards the Kitchen. The Beale family members would

VIEW OF STANDEN FROM THE TOP TERRACE - PHOTO BY KIND PERMISSION OF THE NATIONAL TRUST

rarely have ventured here, in particular the children who in later years would generally greet the housekeeper on their arrival and say goodbye at the end of their stay offering 'thank you's for the nice food they had consumed. Webb's socialist concerns ensured that these rooms were well planned, unlike the poor conditions of many service areas in large Victorian houses. In the Kitchen is the original cast-iron range and it was here that the children's blackberries were weighed to see who had picked the most. The shop now occupies where the Scullery and Cook's Pantry once were and where hours of monotonous labour were passed by those staff present.

You should conclude your visit to Standen by walking in the garden which was unbelievably overgrown, with jungle-like plants when the Trust took over in 1972. You can also see the window of the little room above the Conservatory that Helen Beale is reputed to have asked Webb to build for her (he charged a cost of six pence). In addition on the west side is the second floor window that a long canvas tube was attached to, so that the kids could slide all the way down!

It is perhaps difficult to say that there are no airs of pretension around at Standen. It is after all a very large house to most of us, but none of the rooms are somehow over large or intimidating. It continues to feel a comfortable place, a fact confirmed by the comments of visitors to the house, A number would willingly reside in it, which is probably not always the case with National Trust properties.

On a more negative note, it has also been suggested that its style is not particularly original or progressive for its time. One suggestion is that with its ceiling plaster patterns and the spaciousness of the furniture arrangements it is an example of Georgian revivalism.

It may well be, but it is a shining example of what a combination of artists, craftsmen and other skilled individuals can achieve working to a unified vision.

PART II GAZETTEER

Brighton and Hastings have some of the widest and richest associations with the Pre-Raphaelites and their followers. For this reason I have placed them at the beginning of this gazetteer and those readers for whom time is at a premium, may like to prioritise these trails.

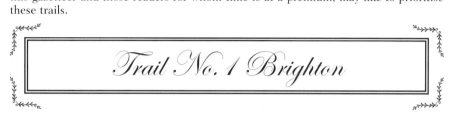

Trail No. 1 Brighton

Points of Interest

(1)   BRIGHTON COLLEGE - Impressive large ensemble of Morris & Co. stained glass in the chapel.****

(2)   CHURCH OF ST. PAUL- Site of early Burne-Jones reredos in Pugin inspired church.*** Also nearby is the address where The Rossetti's stayed in 1850.

(3)   CHURCH OF ST. NICHOLAS - Superior Kempe glass and Morris inspired murals.***

(4)   CHURCH OF ST. MICHAELS AND ALL ANGELS-Important early Morris glass in a building by Bodley with a larger extension by Burges.*****

(5)   HOME OF AUBREY BEARDSLEY

(6)   CHURCH OF ST.PETER- Fine Kempe glass***

(7)   CHURCH OF ST. BARTHOLOMEW- Unique Arts and Crafts inspired decoration****

(8)   CHURCH OF THE ANNUNCIATION- Early Morris glass in the church where Aubrey Beardsley attended.****

(9)   CHURCH OF ST. MARTIN- Glass by Harry Wooldridge and Henry Holiday.***

Also: BRIGHTON ART GALLERY, CHURCH OF ST.AUGUSTINE*** • CHURCH OF ST.PETER, PRESTON PARK** • 17 BRUNSWICK ROAD, HOVE: THE HOUSE WHERE CHRISTINA ROSSETTI STAYED IN 1886 • 23, SECOND AVENUE, HOVE: SITE OF PHILIP WEBB EXTENSION • HOVE ART GALLERY • HOVE CEMETERY • CHURCH OF ST.ANDREW, PORTSLADE***

STARTING POINT: Brighton College is in Eastern Road, a little to the west of the main Royal Sussex County hospital.

HOW TO GET THERE: Eastern Road runs parallel to the A259 coast road, a couple of blocks further inland and on the eastern side of the town. A number of buses serve the area.

FINISHING POINT: Lewes Road in Brighton

REFRESHMENTS: numerous opportunities in town.

TRANSPORT: Best on foot, but cars, buses and taxis can be used.

DURATION: One long day or two days

Although both Hastings and Brighton came in for their own share of criticism from members of the movement, it is Burne-Jones' comments about Brighton that are perhaps the most negative. He generally found Brighton to be 'hateful' and rarely ventured into it from his retreat in Rottingdean.

However, a number of its churches contain important Morris glass and particular note should be given to St. Michael and All Angels with its early examples. In addition, there is some inspired Arts and Crafts work as well as impressive windows by Kempe. Other highlights include the central art gallery which has a number of Pre-Raphaelite paintings and Aubrey Beardsley's childhood home that can be viewed, albeit from the outside.

There are also details about buildings with Pre-Raphaelite connections in the adjacent Hove and Portslade area.

We begin at (1)BRIGHTON COLLEGE *which is located in Kemptown (named after a relative of Charles Eamer Kempe), an area to the east of the city centre.* The college has been on its present site since 1849 although its appearance, at least initially, looks considerably older as it is built in a gothic style associated with the fourteenth century. The architect of the original buildings was Sir George Gilbert Scott with later work by T.G. Jackson who was also a pupil at the college.

Scott's chapel contains no less than thirteen windows with thirty-one separate lights completed by Morris & Co. between 1922-27. These figures do not include the various smaller pieces of glass in the tracery or the rose window at the west end of the nave. Despite the late date of the glass, with many designs being made by John Henry Dearle and other followers of Morris, the effect is visually stunning. This is no doubt due to the high number of designs inhabiting a fairly small space, although the quality does vary, with the original Burne-Jones designs being produced using a form of assembly line, at this late date.

The following descriptions list the windows in a clockwise direction starting to the left of the chapel entrance. It is here in the north aisle that there are three small rectangular windows which are arguably the best in the building. They show *The Adoration of the Magi* (across one whole light) and four smaller depictions of scenes from the life of Christ. They are distinguished by being executed in yellow-stain and pale-grey only, with pale quarries above. They are from Burne-Jones' designs and date from 1924. Following round we see in the aisle's east window, the figures of the saints (left to right) *Thomas, Peter and Matthew.* The first two of these are also from the designs of Burne-Jones with the last figure originating from the pen of Henry Dearle. The next Morris glass is in the east window of the South aisle with four more saints, those of *David, George, Andrew* and *Patrick* - all to Dearle designs dating from 1922. Further saintly figures follow in the next window with three lights of St*ephen, Alban* and *Edmund,* another mix of Burne-Jones and Dearle's work. Moving along there are the allegorical figures of (left to right) *Hope, Charity* and *Faith* against a blue drapery background. These are Burne-Jones again, except for *Charity* which may be by Dearle. Next up and dating from 1924, are *St. Louis* (adapted from Burne-Jones) and King Alfred and Joan of Arc (both Dearle). The aisle's west window is yet more single figures, these being of *St. Christopher* and *St. Francis* by Burne-Jones and Dearle respectively. Interestingly, the first figure is reversed from its original form.

We now re-enter the nave and arrive at a *Nativity* scene which certainly hints at the powerful, sweeping style of Burne-Jones' late work although here it appears perhaps a little cramped. Next door is Dearle's *Sermon on the Mount* which once again lacks the quality of earlier Morris glass, but nevertheless shows great style, produced as it was in

1927. Moving westwards we come to another of Dearle's pictorially styled biblical scenes, the *Ascension of Christ,* from the same year. Finally, there are the windows at the west end, with the musical angels and seraph heads represented in Dearle's rose window installed in 1925. On the left are two further lights, with *Sir Galahad* on the left-hand side against a landscape background. This is interesting for being a design by William Knight who was one of the first tapestry apprentices taken on after Dearle joined the company and who participated in the making of many of the large scale Holy Grail tapestries.

Overall, the chapel offers a golden opportunity to see a wide range of Morris designs within one compact building. ***The visitor should check with the caretaker in regard to access arrangements.***

The suggested route is to now head directly down to the seafront, and go in a westerly direction into town. You will pass the Royal Albion Hotel at the Old Steine (rebuilt following a bad fire) where Oscar Wilde stayed in February 1894. This was three years after he had been introduced to Lord Douglas (Bosie) who was later to live in Hove with his mother. Wilde was a figurehead for the Aesthetic Movement in the 1880's and a great admirer of Burne-Jones' work. It is a sobering thought that he would be dead only six years after being in Brighton following his prison sentence and self imposed exile abroad.

Turning right into West Street you can see the building at number 34 that the

Rossetti family occupied in 1850. Before this on the left, crammed between later buildings is (2) ST. PAUL'S CHURCH. This was designed by R.C Carpenter and built between 1846-8 for the then Vicar of Brighton, Henry Wagner. Like Brighton College, it is also based on a fourteenth century gothic style. The octagonal lantern on the tower was added by Carpenter's son in 1874-5. Inside, its highly decorated state is explained by its roots in The Oxford Movement, the members of which emphasised the ceremonial in their worship. It was this interior that the architect, G.F. Bodley was asked to make additions to in 1861. One of these was for a painted altarpiece in the chancel and Bodley suggested a little known artist of the time to complete this, Edward Burne-Jones. There is some suggestion that another artist who was influential to the early Pre-Raphaelites, William Dyce was asked to do this work but declined perhaps through ill health. Burne-Jones duly produced a triptych depicting the *Adoration of the Magi* with side panels of the *Virgin Mary* and of the *Angel of the Annunciation.* The triptych is no

ST. PAULS CHURCH BRIGHTON - PHOTO BY AUTHOR

*THE LECTERN IN ST PAULS CHURCH
BRIGHTON - PHOTO BY AUTHOR*

longer in the church (except for a smaller reproduction in the narthex)and the story surrounding this is intriguing, if rather convoluted. The first version was considered by the artist to be ' too elaborate to tell its story clearly from a distance' and so a second simplified version was made. This remained in the church until 1975 when it seemed to go out of favour with the church authorities. It was subsequently lent to Brighton Art Gallery but then sadly went to auction and now forms part of the collection of Andrew Lloyd-Webber. Fortunately, the first version was acquired at some point by Bodley who later gave it to the Tate Gallery where it can be frequently viewed. This is well worth doing particularly as the work uses Jane and William Morris, Algernon Swinburne and the artist himself as models for the biblical characters.

The interior today is still of much interest despite the absence of the altarpiece. Under the east window the remnants of the paintings that covered the whole wall can be seen either side of the present reredos. These were completed by a Daniel Bell and presumably would have complemented the Burne-Jones altarpiece. Many of the original fittings were designed by R.C. Carpenter including the painted wooden pulpit. The lectern deserves particular mention with its many angels, designed as it was by Hardman & Co. in the 1880's. The Hardman glass that occupies the main body of the church was designed by Augustus Welby Pugin and has various dates upon it. The later Kempe glass can be seen in what is now the library and the narthex area as you enter the church. *The church is regularly open on weekday mornings.*

Passing No.34, now move up the hill (Queens Road) to Dyke Road and the (3) PARISH CHURCH OF ST. NICHOLAS, Although much of what is seen today dates mainly from the 'restorations' of 1853 and the 1870's, the building has a predominantly fourteenth century tower and contains the best surviving Norman font in the county. But it was the latter 'restoration' that produced much of what can be deemed Pre-Raphaelite. Almost all the stained glass dates from 1870-1886 and is the work of Charles Eamer Kempe, working in a style which occasionally hints at Burne-Jones. The whole story of Christ's life is retold as you move around the interior with his *Childhood* on the south wall and his *Betrayal* appearing opposite. The glass is generally of a high standard although the main east window showing *The Crucifixion* is a little disappointing. This window replaced an earlier one which is now at The Church of The Annunciation and is visited later in this tour. Kempe also painted the roof and the walls of the nave although now only his decoration on the east and west walls survive. The murals on the east wall are particularly interesting as they appear to have been inspired by a Morris design, the flowers of which are in the form of embossed metal. *The church is open on Friday, Saturday and Sunday afternoons.*

When ready head out of the churchyard by the north exit, cross Dyke Road and follow Clifton Terrace into Victoria Road. As you near the (4) CHURCH OF ST. MICHAEL AND ALL ANGELS notice its plain exterior and materials- red and black brick with Bath stone. It was in fact the first brick built church in the town and was quite an innovation. The building was commenced in 1858 and the architect was the ubiquitous G.F.Bodley. His choice of style has been described as French or Italian Gothic and undoubtedly he was influenced by the high profile teachings of Ruskin. Bodley gave the commission for much of the internal decoration to the burgeoning firm then being set up by William Morris and it was their first large scale work.

However, only a few years after the church was completed it proved to be too small for its congregation and an extension was planned. Although this was not completed until 1893, this then dwarfed the original building. Its designer was William Burges although because of his death in 1881 it was completed by his associate, John Chapple.

As you enter the building, the older Bodley church is to the right and this is where the Morris windows are. It is easy to see why Bodley always considered their work here to be their best glass ever produced. Starting in the south east corner, in the Lady Chapel, there is a rare opportunity to observe the stained glass at close quarters. The east window shows on the left, the *Angel of the Resurrection* with the *Three Marys at the Empty Sepulchre* adjacent. Both of these designs show Morris's own work and were his first multi-figure compositions. His *Three Marys* are typical Pre-Raphaelite heroines dressed as they are in long flowing gowns. One of the figures may well have been inspired by a brass rubbing he made in Oxford. The pelican above is by Philip Webb.

DETAIL FROM A KEMPE WINDOW IN THE CHURCH OF ST. NICHOLAS BRIGHTON - PHOTO BY AUTHOR

THE TWO SMALL WINDOWS DEPICTING THE FLIGHT INTO EGYPT IN THE CHURCH OF ST. MICHAEL AND ALL ANGELS IN BRIGHTON - PHOTO BY AUTHOR

Nearby on the south wall is Burne-Jones' *Flight into Egypt* on two small lights which gives some idea of his early mastery of glass design. It was designed to be seen from close quarters and so was drawn with an intimacy and attention to detail. Moving across into what is now the south aisle, you can see to the right a Flemish reredos from the sixteenth century. This was restored by Kempe under Bodley's supervision and is positioned beneath a window containing glass by Clayton & Bell.

Now look directly up and slowly through the gloom the decoration of the ceiling can be observed. This is by Morris, Faulkner and Webb and is thought to have been completed with their own hands. Looking right is the magnificent west window with two lancets showing the figures of saints and a rose window high above surrounded by seven circles. This work has to be one of the greatest earlier achievements of The Firm and includes designs by Burne-Jones, Madox Brown and Morris. Particularly interesting is the depiction of *St. Michael and the Dragon* in the six-foil window above the figures of *St. Michael and St. Raphael* on the left hand side. This is a rare piece of work by Peter Paul Marshall and is full of movement. Only a year or so after this window was installed Marshall almost completely stopped designing windows and returned to work in his career as a surveyor and engineer. Lower down, to the left of this overwhelming window is a smaller gem, consisting of two lights by Burne-Jones and a circle above by Webb. This window commemorates Bodley's father who had died in 1855, but who had been a Brighton doctor living at Merton House in Furze Hill, Hove. It shows *The Baptism of Christ in Jordan*.

Moving into the newer part of the building, amidst all the wonderful stonework, are some features not to be missed. There are choir stalls designed by Burges with

THE COMMEMORATIVE PLAQUE OUTSIDE AUBREY BEARDSLEY'S BIRTHPLACE IN BRIGHTON - PHOTO BY AUTHOR

intriguing misericords, a grey marble font by Bodley, as well as an iron lectern by Kempe. In the north aisle, there are four particularly impressive windows designed by the latter artist, but dating from after his death (1912-16) when the work would have been completed by C.E. Kempe and Co. Ltd. One of these needed much restorative work a few years back following a break-in, when much of the glass was found lying on the floor. The eastern most window in the north aisle is not Kempe's work but a slightly less successful one by a firm called Jones & Willis. This and other Victorian stained glass work on this side of the building (by Clayton & Bell and Worrall) provide a useful counterpoint to the Morris windows.

For a more comprehensive account of all the decorative features in this sumptuous building, there is a good guide available. *Access is limited.*

The trail continues to another ecclesiastical building, the Parish Church of St. Peter. On the way it is possible to view the (5) BIRTHPLACE OF AUBREY BEARDSLEY *at 31 Buckingham Road.* This illustrator and pioneer of the Art Nouveau style has three other connections to the town- he attended Brighton Grammar School in Dyke Road and occasionally stayed with his aunt at 21 Lower Rock Gardens. In addition he attended services at the Church of the Annunciation (see below).

ST. PETER'S CHURCH (6) in Grand Parade (*follow Guildford Road and Trafalgar Street eastwards*), dates from 1828 and has a very famous architect- Charles Barry, who was also responsible for the Houses of Parliament. The building inside is rather austere but has Kempe glass which impresses mainly through its sheer scale. There are a number of his windows on the east side of the nave but these are all inferior to the main north window. Here, against a powerful blue background are many panels of angels, heraldic shields and saints with even a representation of *Queen Victoria* in the bottom right-hand corner. *Christ in Glory* is shown in the centre across three of the five lights. At close quarters the enormous amount of work that went into this window is particularly apparent. Other strong work by Kempe is evident in the chapel with a *Crucifixion* that shows the three crosses, and an Ascent to Calvary. This is superior Kempe work, which does a lot to bolster his reputation against the criticism his glass received in the twentieth century. Finally, the reredos in the chapel has some fine delicate carvings with Pre-Raphaelite inspired angels. *The church is open regularly.*

The next port of call is the unique (7) CHURCH OF ST. BARTHOLOMEW (*found in Ann Street off London Road*). This enormous building (it has been described as 'Noah's Ark and may well be the tallest church in the country) forms part of this itinerary as it is a great showpiece of the Arts and Crafts designer, Henry Wilson. The fittings and interior decoration of the church are inspired by that Movement, which was itself inspired by Morris.

The architect was a local man, Edmund Scott and St. Bartholomew's is easily his most ambitious work. Its style has been described as early Italian Gothic and quite possibly Scott was influenced in this choice by the work of Bodley. The church opened in 1874 but it was not to adopt its present overall appearance for another twenty years or so after this date. Wilson's original designs for the church were even more fantastical than what we now see but nevertheless the church has an interior to take the breath away.

THE ANNUNCIATION WINDOW IN THE CHURCH OF THE SAME NAME IN BRIGHTON - PHOTO BY AUTHOR

In the sanctuary is Wilson's Byzantine inspired baldacchino with its red and green marble. The tabernacle beneath has beaten silver to a design of his and the exquisite altar rails came from his own workshop. There is more repousse work by Wilson in the silver plate of the Lady Altar, featuring the *Adoration of the Magi,* which interestingly replaced an earlier altar by Kempe. Another awesome feature designed by Wilson is the pulpit of Irish marble supported by six columns. Equally pleasing is his font, made with marble again, together with beaten copper. Also of interest but a lot less impressive, are several lancets of stained glass by Kempe & Co. Ltd. who was a business partner with Kempe. *The church is open on most days.*

A walk across The Level brings you to the Hanover district of the city where in Washington Street is the (8) CHURCH OF THE ANNUNCIATION. When the building opened in 1864 this area was very poor but it has now become one of the fashionable places to live in Brighton.

The interior is rather a surprise and contains all manner of unusual artefacts. Immediately inside the door is an attractive relief of the *Annunciation* as well as a stained glass *Transfiguration* in the adjacent tower chapel. Once in the main body of the church there are many panels of glass with single figures of saints but not in a Pre-Raphaelite style. Also in the north aisle (that was added by Edmund Scott, the architect of St. Bartholomew's) is a window to the memory of Pusey and Keble, the founders of the Oxford Movement that was so influential to the building of many Brighton churches.

But it is in the chancel with its rather charming amateurish ceiling decoration that there are good early Morris windows dating from 1866. Here on the left, are shown two angels with organs whilst on the right are a further two, this time carrying harps. In the centre panel at the top are three more of these beautiful creations with their instruments. The *Annunciation* scene beneath is particularly pleasing with the angel *Gabriel* kneeling on the left and the *Virgin* seated facing him. For some reason this window needed repair in 1888 and later in1900 the shape of the window was altered with the installation of the gilt reredos made by Martin Travers. This partially obscures the window but encouragingly, there may be plans to remove it in the near future.

Before leaving take a few minutes to take in the atmosphere of this amazingly quiet church positioned as it is right in the heart of a busy city. It was here that Aubrey

PART OF THE MAIN EAST WINDOW IN ST. MARTINS CHURCH IN BRIGHTON - PHOTO BY AUTHOR

Beardsley indulged his early taste for the High Church when he attended in the company of his sister, Mabel. His early admiration for the work of Burne-Jones might well have come from the times that he knelt in front of the west window. *Access is limited but the church is regularly open on Tuesday mornings.*

A short walk or drive along the Lewes Road will bring you to the lofty (9) ST. MARTIN'S CHURCH dating from 1875. This is another building in which the sheer scale of the whole enterprise takes the breath away. The high interior has an enormous decorated wagon roof with long rows of figures in the clerestory windows just below. These features, together with the glass in the west window, are impressive to look at, but not particularly Pre-Raphaelite in style. This is more evident in the very large reredos at the east end which is reminiscent of church furniture in the major gothic cathedrals of the Low Countries. This one is by Harry Ellis Wooldridge and dates from the time of the completion of the building. Wooldridge also designed the east window high above the reredos which although inevitably viewed from a distance, can be seen to have similarities to early Morris glass. This is not altogether surprising as Wooldridge was working at Powells with Henry Holiday at the time. Indeed, Wooldridge had met Holiday in Burne-Jones' studio during the 1860's and was even Burne-Jones' assistant for a short while. Holiday himself designed two much smaller panels to be seen in the entrance porch and Lady Chapel. *The church is open weekdays from 8-9 am or by arrangement.*

OTHER PLACES OF INTEREST

BRIGHTON ART GALLERY, Church Street.
This recently renovated building houses a large permanent collection, that is particularly strong in items related to design and to the era of Art Nouveau. The gallery also has a number of paintings and drawings done by the Pre-Raphaelites and their associates. Inevitably, these will not always be on show so it is best to check with the staff beforehand and make appropriate arrangements. There are works in the collection by Sandys(a fine Medusa), Beardsley, Brett and Ruskin. In addition, there are a number of pictures by artists who were influenced or inspired by the movement. These include two highly detailed oils by Alma-Tedema, work by Lear (completed whilst abroad and after his painting lessons from Hunt at Fairlight) and a number of watercolours by Hercules B. Brabazon and Frank Brangwyn. There is also a watercolour by Eleanor Brickdale and two from Albert Goodwin including a view of Hastings. Two Burne-Jones studies also form part of the collection with one a charming pastel of a local scene near his home in Rottingdean.

CHURCH OF ST. AUGUSTINE, Stanford Avenue***
This Victorian church has a high impressive interior of brick and stone and an apse at the east end of great originality. It contains one of the best ensembles of Kempe glass in the county. In the south aisle and side chapel there are his windows showing the figures of saints which include *Augustine,* to whom the church is dedicated. These have the makers' marks of the wheatsheaf (generally pre-1907)and the wheatsheaf and the tower. There is also the main east window showing the *Crucifixion* and completed in memory of The Great War. However, it is his small windows in the curve of the apse which most succeed. These include virtues of *Faith, Meekness and Patience* as well as those of *Modesty, Temperance and Chastity.* They date from 1908-21 and are definitely superior work from Kempe & Co. Ltd. **Access is limited.**

CHURCH OF ST.PETER, PRESTON **
Said to have contained a painting of the *Deposition of Christ* by Burne-Jones. This may have been stolen but this has not substantiated.

ADDITIONAL PLACES OF INTEREST IN HOVE

17 BRUNSWICK ROAD, HOVE
The address where Christina Rossetti stayed with her niece in 1886.
23 SECOND AVENUE, HOVE
Philip Webb added a picture gallery to this former house of Constantine Ionides (see below). It survives in an altered condition. Webb also provided Morris and Co. hangings in silk and wool for the house.
HOVE CEMETERY
A little north of the main chapel, in the grounds to the south of the main A27 road, are the graves of Constantine Alexander Ionides and his wife, Agathonike as well as their son, Luke George. They lie beneath one distinctive headstone. Constantine was one of three sons of the successful Greek merchant, Alexander Ionides who was a great patron of Watts, Rossetti and Burne-Jones amongst others. His home at 1,Holland Park, London was the setting for one of the greatest Pre-Raphaelite interiors.

42 THE PANEL PAINTINGS ON THE PULPIT AT ST. ANDREWS CHURCH PORTSLADE - PHOTO BY AUTHOR

Constantine also commissioned work from Philip Webb for his London residence at 8, Holland Villas Road and later at 23 Second Avenue, Hove. He also commissioned Rossetti to paint The Day Dream in 1880.

Immediately west of the chapel by the tarmac road is the grave of William Morris and his wife! This is not of course the William Morris (he is buried near Kelmscott) but interestingly this gothic monument is also in memory of Jane Morris, his daughter. *Access during daylight hours.*

ST. ANDREW'S CHURCH, CHURCH ROAD, PORTSLADE***

This church is the work of Edmund Scott, the architect of St. Bartholomew's but clearly an earlier and far more modest work. This Early English styled building houses a Morris & Co window within its somewhat neglected interior. This is on the south side of the chancel with a dedication to one of the fallen of the First World War. The figure on the left is the allegorical figure of *Valour* from a design by Henry Dearle. *St. Wilfrid* appears on the right in an adapted Burne-Jones design originally depicting St. David.

The pulpit has some interesting panels inserted within it which hopefully will survive intended building work planned in order to incorporate a different use of part of the building. *Access by arrangement.*

HOVE ART GALLERY

Has an early Millais oil in its collection.

Trail No. 2 Hastings to Rye

Points of Interest

(1)   FORMER CHURCH OF ST. MARY MAGDALEN - Burne-Jones stained glass window * * *

ADDRESSES AND LOCATIONS CONNECTED TO THE ROSSETTI FAMILY AND TO GABRIEL ROSSETTI AND LIZZIE SIDDALL

(2)   CHURCH OF ST.CLEMENT-where Gabriel and Lizzie were married, several mementoes in regard to this in the building * * *.

(3)   ALL SAINTS CHURCH - Wall decorations probably by Edward Reginald Frampton and Powell glass * * *.

(4)   HOME OF WHISTLER'S MOTHER

(5)   HASTINGS CEMETERY -Graves of the Whistler family and of Charles Cayley

(6)   FAIRLIGHT-Location of Holman Hunt's ' Our English Coasts'

(7)   WINCHELSEA- the church where Millais worked and the village where he stayed * * *

(8)   RYE - the parish church contains a Burne-Jones window * * *.
    - Lamb House, home of Henry James, an enthusiast of Burne- Jones.

STARTING POINT: St. Margarets Road off Warrior Square, St. Leonards

HOW TO GET THERE Adjacent to main A259

FINISHING POINT: Rye

REFRESHMENTS: Many outlets in Hastings town, pubs at Icklesham and pubs and teashops at Winchelsea and Rye.

TRANSPORT: On foot in Hastings town but car essential thereafter.

DURATION: One full day or two days depending on available time.

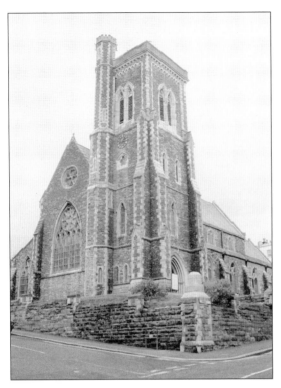

*THE GREEK ORTHODOX CHURCH AT ST. LEONARDS
(FORMERLY THE CHURCH OF ST.MARY MAGDALEN) -
PHOTO BY AUTHOR*

The first part of this trail is based in Hastings and St. Leonards and it then moves eastwards stopping at villages and other locations to end in Rye, twelve miles away. If arriving by car from the west you pass an area known as Bo Peep which is helpfully sign-posted by the pub of the same name on the left hand side. It was in this vicinity that John Keats the poet and great inspiration for many Pre-Raphaelites stayed in 1817.

The tour commences in St. Leonards, the town created from the 1820's by a London builder, James Burton with his son Decimus as his architect. It is now fused together with Hastings into one large urban area.

Walk through Warrior Square to St. Margarets Road which runs in an easterly direction from the square. There is a Greek Orthodox Church on the left as the road begins to rise. Formally this was (1)THE CHURCH OF ST MARY MAGDALEN and it contains a Morris window of 1881 featuring the *Mary Virgin* and *St. Elizabeth* which is found in the south aisle. Currently the building is being restored and clearly the tracery at the top of the window has had some repair comparatively recently. With one or two exceptions the other windows are by Clayton & Bell and date from 1870, unfortunately those on the west side were destroyed in the last war including, it is said, a rather fine version of the *Te Deum.*

It was here in 1897 that the Rev. C. L. Dodgson gave an address to the congregation on the occasion of Harvest Festival. This was none other than Lewis Carroll, the creator of Alice in Wonderland and also the man responsible for some of the most familiar photographs of Rossetti, Ruskin and other members of the Pre-Raphaelite circle. *The church is unfortunately locked some of the time but you may be lucky and gain entry.*

Now, head down towards Carlisle Parade on the seafront. In Victorian times, Hastings was a popular destination for those seeking a cure for illness or recuperation afterwards, as well as for a holiday. Throughout their lives members of the Rossetti family came down from London to do this and it was on one of these occasions that Christina stayed at NO.2 CARLISLE PARADE (now the Hotel Europa). *Now head eastwards along the seafront to arrive shortly at the site of another of the boarding*

houses Christina stayed at, this time in the company of her mother in April 1873. Sadly, 17 ROBERTSON TERRACE is now gone, replaced by Albany Court to the left of the Debenhams store. From here Christina wrote to Gabriel who was staying with Jane Morris at Kelmscott-

'Dearest Mamma is very well again, and wonderfully well in her feet, which now bear her about in comfort. I am very well too, all things considered. Winter has been with us again, but today gives hopes of spring or summer to come. A Bath chair is to come for me at 12:30, to take me out for the first time since our coming down.'

Christina may well have also been concerned for the health of her sister Maria, who was in Sussex at this time. She was recuperating from an illness in Eastbourne (see Trail No.5).

If you continue to proceed east past todays amusement arcades, the Old Town of Hastings is reached. Before this a popular pub called THE CUTTER at what used to be 12 East Parade bears a blue heritage plaque and this commemorates the building Rossetti found lodgings in prior to his wedding in 1860. His room may well have been where the saloon bar is now. A little further along is a part of the front called EAST BEACH STREET and it was here at 12 Beach Houses at the same time that Lizzie Siddall was very unwell and so the wedding had to be delayed. Most of the older houses

have disappeared but there are one or two buildings which still give some idea of that bow windowed house that in 1860 was lashed with sea spray when the wind was at the back of the incoming tide.

In this area you will notice the STAVES which are the tall dark wooden structures used for storage by the local fishermen. This is the old fishing quarter immortalised in Christina's story 'Vanna's Twins' where a man makes his livelihood by 'picking up marine oddities, pebbles, or weeds'. She was also concerned with the lives of ordinary impoverished fishermen and their families in 'The Waves of this Troublesome World'.

After looking around this interesting area you can walk up to or ride in the lift to the East Hill, the place used by Gabriel and Lizzie in the first days of their romance when Lizzie's health permitted. It commands fine views over the town.

Then retrace your steps to find the High Street heading north from the seafront. This is

NO. 2 CARLISLE PARADE HASTINGS - PHOTO BY AUTHOR

THE CUTTER PUB IN HASTINGS - PHOTO BY AUTHOR

THE PLAQUE WITH REPRODUCTION OF THE PAINTING 'ECCE ANCILLA DOMINI' BY DANTE GABRIEL ROSSETTI IN ST. CLEMENTS CHURCH, HASTINGS - PHOTO BY AUTHOR

the main thoroughfare of the Old Town and has an abundance of antique and secondhand shops. Shortly you will notice (2) ST. CLEMENT'S CHURCH up a flight of steps to your left. On 23rd. May 1860 Lizzie and Gabriel were wed here although the register gives the poet's Christian name as Daniel. The only other people present were the minister and the caretaker of the church with his wife, who probably acted as witnesses. *The church is often open* and once inside you should turn immediately to the left where a memorial to the poet is situated. This is in the form of a reproduction of his early painting 'Ecce Ancilla Domini!' (or The Annunciation of 1850).This copy was unveiled in 1928. One should also see the lamp containing the ever burning flame which is in the chancel close to the altar. It bears the names of Gabriel and Lizzie around the outside.

Upon leaving this delightful church recommence your journey up the High Street looking for No. 81 *on the right.* Christina stayed here in 1865 with her cousin Henrietta Polydore who was suffering from the common Victorian malady, consumption. In fact Christina at this time also had a very persistent cough which gave cause for concern that she might be developing the illness.

Continuing northwards you will soon reach NO.9 which is the location for one of the earliest Rossetti connections with Hastings. It was here that Gabriel's father came following poor health in June 1843. Two doors away is

NO. 5, a former boarding house where Gabriel scandalously moved in to be with Lizzie in the early days of their courtship.

The poet Coventry Patmore who was supportive of the work of the Pre-Raphaelites and provided the subject matter for a number of their important works, lived for a number of years at MANSION HOUSE on the left at the top of the street.

The next stop is provided by (3)ALL SAINTS CHURCH high up on a mound *on the other side of the main A259 at the end of the High Street.* Inside this building, there is attractive Powell glass at the west end of the south aisle and in the north aisle. In the former window only the centre light remains with more recent glass either side. The two windows in the opposite aisle commemorate members of the Foyster family and date from 1897 and 1911 and reflect a time when Morris's influence was still important in the work of the Powell firm.

There is further glass by Clayton & Bell amongst others but the greatest interest is provided by the decorations in the chancel that form a reredos. These are likely to be by Edward Reginald Frampton and date from around 1905. Frampton has been referred to as 'a younger Burne-Jones' and his style is very decorative and rather mannered in a similar way. He was an enthusiastic sailor and so many of his works show marine connections although this is not apparent in the reredos. Nevertheless, his angels are quite distinctive and the ones in this church can be compared to those depicted in his oil paintings. *The church is sometimes locked but access is possible through contact with the church rector.*

The rest of the trail is best completed using your own transport. In order to reach the HOUSE OF WHISTLER'S MOTHER (4) from 1876 - 1881, *go up Queens Road and then cut through the back streets to reach St. Marys Terrace with its fine views.* Although Whistler is not classed as a Pre-Raphaelite he was very much a contemporary

VIEW OF HASTINGS FROM THE ONCE HOME OF WHISTLER'S MOTHER - PHOTO BY AUTHOR

of Burne-Jones and shared with him an interest in the purely aesthetic qualities of art. At number 43 there is a plaque beneath the bay window informing passers-by of his mother's dates of residence. It has been suggested that the artist actually painted the world famous portrait of his mother (*Arrangement in Grey and Black* 1871) inside although this is unlikely because it is dated some five years before. There is a story of how the curtains and stool in the painting were preserved in the house for years afterwards but the current owner alas does not know their whereabouts! However Whistler did visit his mother here and no doubt painted and sketched whilst in the town.

From the house head back through the Victorian terraces to pick up the St. Helens Road which is also the A2101 heading out to Ore. After passing the Alexandra Park on your left you will shortly arrive at a junction with Sedlescombe Road where you should look to your right for OLD ROAR ROAD *and continue down it.* Although this area has been redeveloped on a number of occasions since the middle of the nineteenth century you will soon arrive at some older buildings. A house on the right is called Old Roar and bears the date 1862 whilst another nearby is 1867 and a little further on is the larger Old Roar House. It is difficult to substantiate if Rossetti stayed in this particular house but it is relatively easy to imagine this vicinity at the end of the last century to be an attractive and secluded place only a short distance from central Hastings. He and Lizzie scratched their initials on a stone at this location and gave directions to this in a letter to his mother of the 1st. July 1855-

'Our stone would lie to your right as you stood with your back to the fall, a little way in front of you. By the bye, the fall seems to have fallen most completely and successfully, for we couldn't see it.'

Evidently the place was already changing in those days, so there is little likelihood of seeing any actual evidence of their stay but some of the atmosphere lives on.

It is now only a couple of miles or so to the (5) MAIN CEMETERY *along The Ridge road.* This is the burial place of Whistler's mother Anna Matilda who died in 1881, aged 74.In addition, his brother William McNeill Whistler who had been a surgeon in the Confederate Army during the American Civil war lies here with his wife Helen. Whistler took long walks with his brother and sister-in-law near Hastings Castle before attending his mother's funeral. He is also said to have been concerned at the time that he had been a disappointment to his mother-

'It would have been better had I been a parson as she wanted'.

Local rumour has it that Whistler himself may have been buried next to his mother and his wife. Apparently fans of the artist have been known to make the long journey from Massachusetts to visit his last resting place, but they would almost definitely be looking in the wrong place here. Certainly the family graves recorded in the name of Whistler were in an area which has subsequently been converted into the Garden of Rest. However it is recorded that Whistler himself was actually buried in Chiswick Cemetery on the 23rd. July 1903.

A grave that can be seen is that of Sophia Cayley who was the sister of the linguist Charles Bagot Cayley who is buried in the same grave. He was the subject of Christina Rossetti's second affair of the heart (the first being James Collinson, a painter and member of The Brotherhood who later retired to a monastery) although when he finally proposed to her in 1866 she declined, the reason given being religious differences. He died on the 12th. December 1883 and his grave was visited by Christina who was most traumatised by the death of a man with whom she always maintained a devoted friendship. Her revised poem 'One Seaside Grave' is almost definitely about this sad event. There is now only a rather lonely solitary pine tree that appears to mark the

ECCLESBOURNE GLEN - PHOTO BY AUTHOR

location of the grave *which is to be found on plot AD (no. A4).* At the time of writing the gravestone has fallen over underlining its neglect, perhaps now there is no one to remember. There is another family stone nearby and if you have time you should have a stroll around, there is a certain ambience with a fine view from the back over an area that extends towards Fairlight, another famous location for the Pre-Raphaelites.

Now head that way via The Ridge, Old London Road and Fairlight Road to stop at the top of Fairlight Avenue. Here it is possible to walk over to (6) FAIRLIGHT GLEN using footpaths that pass through some very pleasant countryside and then return using an alternative path. After a couple of miles or so the beach will be reached but on the way it is worth looking out for Ecclesbourne Glen between Fairlight and Hastings. This would appear to be a contender for the place where Holman Hunt painted 'Our English Coasts' (see colour illustration) particularly with its close proximity to the site of Clive Vale Farm where he stayed in the company of Edward Lear. No doubt the coastline here has changed a great deal since the 1850's with erosion and different vegetation, but on a sunny day the painting could almost be recreated.

It is documented that Hunt worked from a beauty spot called The Lover's Seat, further along the coast overlooking Covehurst Bay, but the painting has a number of differing viewpoints gained throughout the area so it is perhaps unsurprising that the essence of the painting is felt repeatedly whilst in this landscape. Lover's Seat was also the location for a number of Rossetti sketches of Lizzie Siddal and vice versa in 1854.

In the early 1870's Walter Crane also found his heart was at Fairlight 'where a certain lady was staying' - his future wife and he writes about how 'quickly fled those summer days by the sparkling sea'. Frederick Sandys, another artist and occasional friend of Rossetti was also drawn to work in this area in 1870. He is now best known for his black and white illustrations to popular magazines of the 1860's as well as paintings of mythological women. Also nearby but not really visible, is Fairlight Lodge, the home of the painter Robert Martineau's parents and there are a number of family graves in the local churchyard.

A poet of the time, William Wilson should perhaps have the last word on this beautiful place which has lost only a little of its charm since he wrote in 1860-

'For when thou hast donn'd thy soft mantle of green,
Thou art grand in thy solitude -sweet Fairlight Glen!'

Heading eastwards again make your way to (7) WINCHELSEA, *you might choose to go via the village of Pett and then use the minor road called Pannel Lane. This cannot fail but give a better idea of the countryside in earlier times than a trip along the main A259. On arrival the ancient church soon appears on your right.* The CHURCH OF ST THOMAS may be a shadow of its former self and from the outside it is difficult to decide if it was ever completed, but undoubtedly still has grandeur. Inside, one is first overwhelmed by the stunning stained glass - not Pre-Raphaelite but designed by Douglas Strachan in the 1920's. Interestingly, in the appreciation booklet written by his daughter (available in the church) she is at odds to point out that her father's inspiration was his own and not Burn Jones (sic) as others have suggested.

It was here inside the church that Millais painted his picture 'L'Enfant du Regiment' otherwise known as 'The Random Shot'. in October and November of 1854. This was during his second and longer visit to the town where he stayed for over three months. He had previously visited in August two years before in the company of Hunt and Edward Lear whilst they were engaged in working at Fairlight. Look on the right-hand side for the fourteenth century effigy of Gervaise Alard upon which the painting depicts a young girl lying down. The subject of the picture has been accidentally wounded in fighting during the French wars of the First Republic after being orphaned and adopted by a regiment. This story is based on the opera by Donizetti entitled 'La Fille du Regiment' which Millais could have seen performed in London in 1847-8 or 1850-1. The figure of the child was not painted in the church but added a year later at Millias's home in Perth, Scotland. He used the same model for one of the characters in 'The Blind Girl' (see colour illustration) arguably amongst his greatest works, and also partially completed at Winchelsea.

This shows a blind beggar girl and her companion sitting down in open countryside waiting for a shower to clear. It also highlights a social problem of its day and has an

'SWEET THOUGHTS' BY FREDERICK SANDYS (1894) - PERMISSION OF WORTHING MUSEUM AND ART GALLERY

emotional pull in its beautiful and accurate depiction of landscape and the fact that the girl can see none of it. Although the figures (the older model was not Effie Millais as has been suggested) and foreground were painted in Perth, the town of Winchelsea is faithfully reproduced shown from fields to the east. When Millais started the work in August 1854 he wrote to the poet Alfred Lord Tennyson to say that he was *'intending to stay until it is too unseasonable to sit out of doors'*. The result was a picture that is a prime example of a Pre-Raphaelite landscape with its high degree of detail and wonderful luminosity. Rossetti and Ruskin particularly loved and admired it, despite the twin rainbow being originally painted incorrectly with both arcs in the same order of colours. Millais later corrected this to show the reflected arc in reverse.

Nowadays if you walk down beside the Royal Military canal (there is a footpath that leads along it from Strand Bridge on the A259 going onwards towards Rye) you can get some idea of the location of the painting. Without jumping over drainage channels you cannot get back as far as Millais did, but the ancient Strand Gate is still visible as is the high roofed building to its right. The church and other buildings are now hidden behind the trees and bushes growing on Friars Cliff.

In October 1866 Rossetti came to Winchelsea whist on a walking tour with Frederick Sandys. Their friendship was always a little fiery and it seems that an argument occurred which contributed to a rift between the two men. They later made this up but a number of years passed by with only minimal contact taking place.

Walter Crane also visited the town with his wife and children in the spring of 1890 and found it and the neighbouring country *'all full of attraction for us'*. Whilst in this part of the world, take a longer look at this lovely town where Coventry Patmore and Thackeray wrote and where Ellen Terry, the Victorian actress resided at Tower Cottage. **Winchelsea church is open most days.**

TOMB OF GERVAISE ALARD IN WINCHELSEA CHURCH - PHOTO BY AUTHOR

Heading onwards along the A259 you will soon come to the delightful hilltop town of (8) RYE *close to the Sussex/Kent county boundary.* Amongst the many book and tea shops is the CHURCH OF ST. MARY which in terms of sheer size is more like a cathedral. The view from the top of its embattled tower is quite exhilarating.

As you enter the nave turn to your right and look for the window in the north aisle , second in from the west end of the church. This is Burne Jones's *Adoration of the Magi* completed in 1897 from his design of 1885 and first used at Easthampstead. It shows the *Holy Family* in the right hand light and angels in the foreground, with the story retold over both lights. Craftsmen from the Morris workshop involved with the production of the window included such lesser luminaries as Messrs. Dearle, Titcomb, Walters and Stokes. The inscription by Campfield commemorates members of the Tiltman family.

There are also some fine windows by Kempe in the south aisle although the Burne Jones glass is difficult to leave. *The church is open most days.*

Close by is LAMB HOUSE, the home of the writer Henry James from 1897 until his death in 1916. It was here that he wrote a number of his most accomplished works including *The Wings of the Dove*. At the time of his residence the house would have been decorated with, amongst other Victorian artists' paintings, works by Burne-Jones. James was a great admirer of his work and although there are now no examples of his work in the house there is a portrait of James by Philip Burne-Jones dating from 1894. *The house is in the care of the National Trust and is open to the public from April to October on Thursday and Saturday from 2-6.*

TODAYS VIEW OF THE LOCATION FOR MILLAIS'S 'THE BLIND GIRL' - PHOTO BY AUTHOR

A DETAIL OF BURNE - JONES' ADORATION OF THE MAGI IN THE CHURCH OF ST. MARY IN RYE - PHOTO BY AUTHOR

Trail No. 3 On the borders of Kent

Points of Interest

(1)   SALEHURST CHURCH- Stained glass by Kempe**

(2)   HURST GREEN CHURCH-Decorated interior inspired by Morris***

(3)   SCALANDS FARM -Former property used by Barbara Bodichon and visited by Rossetti at different times of his life, with both Lizzie Siddall and Jane Morris

(4)   NETHERFIELD CHURCH-High Victorian interior **

(5)   SEDLESCOMBE CHURCH-Kempe glass and connections to the artist, Hercules Brabazon **

Also: BEXHILL - CHURCH OF ST. STEPHEN - Stained glass by Harry Mileham*** and the CHURCH OF ST. PETER - Pre-Raphaelite styled murals ***.

STARTING POINT: Salehurst church.

HOW TO GET THERE: Salehurst is sign-posted from the A21 just north of Robertsbridge.

FINISHING POINT: Sedlescombe village

REFRESHMENTS: Shops at Hurst Green, Sedlescombe. Pubs at Salehurst, Sedlescombe

DURATION: Morning / afternoon or a leisurely full day.

The (1) CHURCH OF ST. MARY THE VIRGIN contains a formidable array of both Victorian glass and windows from later periods. However, the window to look out for has to be that in the Lady Chapel which the church guide describes as a 'most noteworthy window by Kempe, the Pre-Raphaelite artist'. Although perhaps not one of his very best, it is pleasing enough with a nice central panel showing the *Three Virtues*.

Also of interest in the foyer area is some information about The Lover's Seat at Fairlight, the beauty spot chosen by Holman Hunt as the location for *Our English Coasts*. *The church is open regularly.*

Leave the church by continuing to go further along the same minor road you came in on. After taking the left turn at a T junction the A21 is found again, turn right and you will arrive at Hurst Green where the (2) CHURCH OF THE HOLY TRINITY *is to be seen a little hidden, on the left hand side of the main road.*

Although this church has no connections with William Morris or his associates, its amazing decorative scheme is certainly inspired by him. The painted walls have panels with subjects such as the *Signs of The Passion* below appropriate painted verse. There are also lilies, grapes and vestments shown in addition to *The Trinity* after which of course the building is named. There is a painted ceiling in the chancel with decorated roof bosses and pleasant foliage designs. A notice in the porch attributes the decorative

THE VIEW TODAY FROM SCALANDS FARMHOUSE - PHOTO BY AUTHOR

work to a 'Mrs Carter of The Lodge' and dates the work to 1906 with further work paid for by Mr and Mrs Brookes-Smith of the same address, four years later.

The glass in the church is okay if unremarkable, and not particularly complimentary to the murals. **The church is sometimes locked but access can be obtained easily by contacting the local church warden.**

The next stop is Scalands Farm but before heading there it is possible to view GLOTTENHAM MANOR, *(off a minor road south of Robertsbridge)* where there are a number of farm buildings nearby, one of which Christina Rossetti stayed at in 1872. She was in the company of her mother at a bad time when all the members of the Rossetti family were experiencing varying degrees of illness. Christina's health improved here and she was able to play croquet, although she could not do this for long as her feet became swollen. The present manor house (now a nursing home) bears a later date than that of Christina's visit but some of the other buildings were no doubt in existence in 1872. Whilst convalescing, Barbara Bodichon asked her over to Scalands and although Christina was a little anxious in her presence, she did visit and enjoyed this change of surrounding.

This is indeed the next stop on this trail, so **return to Robertsbridge High Street where in the centre of the town go right to the railway station which is also the road to Brightling. Beyond the station and after a sharp turn to the left (3) SCALANDS FARM is signed to the left. This is a public right of way so park carefully and then walk down. After passing a smallholding you will see the farm directly in front of you, the footpath skirts it to the right.** Although the buildings are private property it is easy to appreciate the fine far reaching views that open out on both sides. In the far distance down the valley on the left can be seen the tower of Salehurst church. The scene is rather evocative of the days Rossetti spent walking and sketching in the company of Lizzie Siddal and (separately) Jane Morris as well as William Stillman and Barbara Bodichon.

You should now retrace your steps back to your car and continue along the road in the same direction as before. Passing through Twelve Oaks and Cackle Street you join the B2096 and a short distance further on there is a turnoff to Netherfield where the church later appears on your left. The (4) CHURCH OF ST. JOHN THE BAPTIST dates from 1860 and was designed by S.S. Teulon, a somewhat maverick,

Victorian architect. He was also responsible for the buildings close by including a school and parsonage. The interior of the church is full of his unusual fittings such as the spiky reredos and stone pulpit together with the exuberant octagonal font. These features together with the chandeliers and other furniture, help create a Gothic styled space that would be a familiar backdrop to many Pre-Raphaelite artworks, offset as it is by the west window which betrays a Morris like inspiration. ***The church is open most days.***

The final destination of this short trail is another ST. JOHN THE BAPTIST CHURCH (5), this one being in the village of Sedlescombe. ***Continue along the minor road to Battle and look out for a turning on your left off the High Street, this will take you to Sedlescombe via Whatlington. The church will appear on the left.*** The building received a major 'restoration' in 1838 when it was enlarged, mainly at the instigation of a John Pratt who is still the longest serving rector for the Parish. The main east window is in his memory, and shows the *Last Supper* and *Crucifixion* in an unusually detailed, non naturalistic way and for which no designer is known. Amid the High Victorian furnishings (more 'restoration' work was completed in 1874) are a stone and marble pulpit, a carved reredos, as well as a low iron screen. There is also a magnificent sixteenth century font cover with doors that fold back, another feature which along with windows by Kempe help to evoke a Pre-Raphaelite feel to this interior. The Kempe windows are in the chancel and quite good for their date (1890).

Of most interest is the Oaklands Corner of the church located in the west end of the south aisle. Here there are memorials to members of the Brabazon Sharpe family who lived at nearby Oaklands House which was built by Decimus Burton in the 1830's. The painter, Hercules Brabazon Brabazon lived there throughout his life and in 1867 was elected for membership to the Burlington Fine Arts Club at the same time as

PART OF THE VICTORIAN MURAL IN ST. PETERS CHURCH IN OLD BEXHILL - PHOTO BY AUTHOR

Rossetti and Ruskin. In 1880 he accompanied Ruskin and others on a sketching tour of Amiens.

Brabazon's watercolours can in no way be called Pre-Raphaelite but his practice of using bodycolours directly onto tinted paper was influential for both Whistler and Albert Goodwin. In addition, Ruskin thought him a highly accomplished colourist. *The church is open most days.*

DETAIL OF STAINED GLASS BY HARRY MILEHAM IN ST. STEPHENS CHURCH IN WOODSGATE PARK BEXHILL - PHOTO BY AUTHOR

If you wish to return to Salehurst retrace your previous route as far as the intersection with the A21 and then head northwards along it.

The Asburnham estate where Algernon Swinburne spent some of his early days is relatively nearby where the church can be visited and the grounds are occasionally open.

ALSO: In the town of Bexhill nearby are two further churches worthy of note.

Found in the old village of Bexhill, a little inland from the present town centre is the CHURCH OF ST. PETER. This church has a remarkable set of wall paintings in the chancel. They show biblical characters on the north side and a charming *Nativity* opposite. Above these are Morrisian angels and even higher, a nicely decorated ceiling. These were completed in the mid-1890's by a man who was presumably local, W. G. Rich. The work has a dark mystery to it and the Powell window showing a number of angels (in the north-east corner) struggles to illuminate it. Elsewhere in the building is glass by Clayton & Bell (in the main east window), Heaton, Butler & Bayne (signed and in the south aisle) and Powells again in the Lady Chapel. *The church is open most weekday afternoons and at other times by contact with the church wardens.*

In the Woodsgate Park area of the town is the relatively unknown CHURCH OF ST. STEPHEN built at the end of the nineteenth century.

The prime reason for visiting are the two windows by the local latter day Pre-Raphaelite, Harry Mileham. The large window in the south transept is particularly wonderful. It dates rather incredibly from 1934-6 although in style it could be fifty years earlier. It has six scenes from the *Life of St. Stephen* within its two long lancets, each with two lights. Even on a dull day it appears bright (especially in comparison to the dull Powell like glass elsewhere in the building) but the glass is never gaudy, with the figures very lifelike. In the south chapel there is further work by Mileham but not to quite the same standard. This is also signed with a date of 1935, having scenes of the *Nativity* on clear quarried panels.

The church is often locked but access is possible through contact with the church wardens.

Trail No. 4 Mid Sussex

Points of Interest

(1) LINDFIELD-All Saints Church - Kempe glass ***
- Old Place, Kempe's Home

(2) HAYWARDS HEATH - Church of St. Wilfrid-small Morris windows in a building by Bodley***

(3) CUCKFIELD - Church of The Holy Trinity-unique Kempe decorated ceiling and windows***

(4) STAPLEFIELD - Church of St. Mark-murals by Kempe, very much in the style of Morris***

(5) SLAUGHAM - Parish Church-more Kempe glass including a rose window**

(6) HORSHAM - St. Mary's Church has an abundance of nineteenth century stained glass ***

(7) CHRIST'S HOSPITAL - Woolner sculpture and Brangwyn paintings

(8) LOWFIELD HEATH - Church of St. Michael - unusual Burges designed building****

STARTING POINT: The village of Lindfield manages to maintain its own individual identity despite there being no obvious division between it and the commuter belt sprawl of Haywards Heath. The church is located to the north of the village on the eastern side.

HOW TO GET THERE: Follow the road northwards out of Haywards Heath signposted from the A272.

FINISHING POINT: Lowfield Heath village adjacent to Gatwick airport

REFRESHMENTS: Many opportunities in the towns of Haywards Heath, Cuckfield and Horsham.

TRANSPORT: Car essential.

DURATION: Full day

ALL SAINTS CHURCH (1) in Lindfield was twice restored by the Victorians. C. E. Kempe was much involved on the second occasion, not surprisingly as he was the resident of nearby Old Place (visible to the east of the churchyard). He was instrumental in providing the chancel screen you see today which dates from the 1880's. Amidst the sea of stained glass are some superior delights. Firstly, there is the window in the north transept by Kempe & Co. Ltd. which actually commemorates the baptism of Walter Tower's daughter. In the south chapel is another strong window with the combined monogram of the wheatsheaf and tower. This shows the figures of *St. George* and *St. Michael with the Virgin and Child*. Also of interest is the west window in the same chapel which was designed by Christopher Whall in 1906 and has an intensity similar to Holman Hunt in its representation of a cornfield. *The church is open most days.*

As you leave the building have a glimpse of Kempe's old abode which has his garden pavilion to the rear of it.

Now head into Haywards Heath and just before the roundabout with the A272 take the road on the right. On the left, the large outline of the (2) CHURCH OF ST. WILFRID *will soon appear.* It was built by Bodley between 1863-5 and despite the loss and replacement of its main east window still contains a number of small Morris windows. After entering the lofty interior it is worth spending a few minutes imagining what this would have been like prior to 1962 when the Morris & Co. window was destroyed. In its three lights there would have been three tiers of subjects that were surrounded by decorative quarries. On the upper tier were the figures of *Mary the Virgin, Christ on the Cross* and *St. John* all to designs by Burne-Jones. In the centre tier were three scenes relating to the *Nativity* also by Burne-Jones, whilst below there were two scenes of the *Annunciation* by him as well as a dove designed by Philip Webb.

Moving from imagination to reality there are still a number of small windows to be seen in the chancel, baptistery and nave. High up on the south side of the chancel are the figures of *St. Raphael, St. Wilfrid* and *St. Michael*. In the baptistery window there are two lights with *Moses* and *St. Peter* on the left side and *Noah* and *St. Paul* on the right. These all date from 1867 whilst the three pairs of windows showing the figures of saints in the south aisle of the nave are three years later. Curiously you will notice a fourth window showing *St. Elizabeth* and *Zacharias* that appears to have been made to match the other three but was in fact made by the company of Scott & Garner in 1878. The figures lack haloes and their skin hues are lighter. The figures of *St Alban* and *St James the Greater* from the Morris workshop have been replaced in recent years presumably following vandalism. *The church is open regularly.*

Next stop is (3) THE CHURCH OF THE HOLY TRINITY at Cuckfield. *Follow the A272 out of town and continue westwards until the village is reached; the church is on the left hand side.* Bodley also worked here restoring the building in 1855-6. Kempe, his pupil, as we know lived nearby and occasionally worshipped here. He was responsible for the design of the south porch in 1883 as well as a number of stained glass windows. However it is his decoration of the ceilings in the church that are justifiably well praised. These wagon form roofs were completed by 1886. There are also four windows by Kempe including a *Tree of Jesse* on the west wall of the north aisle dating from 1887. In the south aisle are contrasting windows by the rival firms of Ward and Hughes and Clayton and Bell. *The church is open regularly.*

More murals by Kempe are to be found in (4) ST. MARK'S CHURCH in Staplefield. *To get there head northwards out of the village, then take the B2114 on the left. On arrival at Staplefield green take the right turn and shortly afterwards*

THE MURAL BY KEMPE IN STAPLEFIELD CHURCH IS VERY MORRIS LIKE IN STYLE - PHOTO BY AUTHOR

the church appears on the left. The building was consecrated in 1847 shortly after the arrival of the railway to Sussex. This had resulted in a great influx of people to this area with a resultant need for further places of worship. The architect was Benjamin Ferrey and his finished work with its three tier bellcote has an uncomplicated simplicity. The interior houses all manner of interesting artefacts, many of which have a connection with the Messel family from nearby Nymans.

The chapel at the west end has a memorial to members of this prestigious family as well as other furnishings including an oak screen and a banner, donated by them. Also here is a Kempe window of 1897 showing *John the Baptist* and commemorating the first fifty years of the churches' life. If we continue down the south aisle passing an interesting sculpture of *St. Sebastian* and some Clayton & Bell windows we arrive at the chancel.

Here are Kempe's murals on the north, south and east walls with further decoration on the ribs of the roof. They are a splendid sight and without doubt very Morris in style. They show angels against trees and other foliage with further angels with heraldic shields on the east wall. Unfortunately the decoration on the north wall is partially obscured by the organ and the lower part of the murals have been painted over, as can be seen by looking underneath the choir seating. Nevertheless they still delight the eye. They date from 1866-74 and cost a princely £74 at the time.

The main east window replaced an earlier one in 1918 and again commemorates members of the Messel family. The three slim lancets show standard saint figure designs with *Christ in Majesty* in the centre light and a wheatsheaf/tower emblem can be seen on the left. They are a little disappointing in their auspicious surroundings.

Continuing in an anti-clockwise direction we pass a nice Victorian pulpit with granite columns and two lancets with designs that are probably by Powells and dated 1901. Be sure not to miss the unusual font with its appropriate inscription *'Suffer the little children to come unto me'*.

Our next visit on this trail (that is full of Kempe's work)is (5) SLAUGHAM CHURCH. *Take the road that leaves Staplefield green on the south-west side and follow this under the A23 to Slaugham where the church is on your left.*

Inside, on the north wall nearest the tower, is a Kempe window in memory of a Warden Sergison. Amongst the nice detailing is an impressive devil as well as two finely observed figures in armour. To the left of the south porch screen is another good Kempe window but pride of place must go to the rose window on the west wall. Here we have Pre-Raphaelite angels as well as the *Instruments of the Passion* in a most agreeable design. Before leaving, the Richard Covert monument of 1579 can be viewed as should carving on the Flemish pulpit of 1890. *The church is open most days.*

The (6) CHURCH OF ST. MARY THE VIRGIN in Horsham should be mentioned in passing, *(follow the A279, then turn right along the A281)* as it contains a

A DETAIL OF THE MESSEL WINDOW BY KEMPE IN STAPLEFIELD CHURCH - PHOTO BY AUTHOR

veritable visual dictionary of Victorian stained glass in its windows. Designs by Lavers, Barraud & Westlake, Powells and Wailes can be viewed alongside more Pre-Raphaelite inspired work by Heaton, Butler & Bayne. There is also a window in the Holy Trinity Chapel that originates in the Kempe workshops but is designed by H.W.Bryans and contains his signatory sable hound courant. *The church is open for a limited time on most days.*

Just outside Horsham is (7) CHRIST'S HOSPITAL, a school that was designed by Sir Aston Webb between 1893 and 1902. In the chapel are a number of interesting murals by Frank Brangwyn, who had previously worked in the Morris shop in Oxford Street in 1882-4. On the staircase leading to the museum (*open Wed., Thurs., Fri., 2-5 during term*) in the old infirmary block is a copy of the sculpture called *The Coleridge Memorial Prize* by Thomas Woolner. Completed in 1875 this is a comparatively rare example of Pre-Raphaelite sculpture. It shows the figures of three ex-pupils of the school, namely Coleridge, Thomas Middleton and Charles Lamb. A copy of this small work is given annually to the winner of the school's literary prize.

Woolner is also said to be responsible for the four figures beneath the fountain in the central court of the school.

The final but no less worthy destination of this trail lies within a few yards of the main runway of Gatwick Airport. *Go east along the A264 and turn left at the junction with the A23.* The village of Lowfield Heath (sign-posted) has now all but disappeared under a welter of airport warehouses and hotels that now surround the (8) CHURCH OF ST. MICHAEL AND ALL ANGELS. But this bizarre setting provides the backdrop to one of the most original churches in the county. Built in 1868 this building is a rare example of the work of William Burges, a gothic inspired

ARMORIAL FIGURES BY KEMPE AT SLAUGHAM CHURCH - PHOTO BY AUTHOR

architect who knew Morris and Burne-Jones well and with whom he occasionally collaborated. Burges is responsible for the outside decoration of the church as well as its unique interior which both contain a number of carvings. The exterior of the large west facing rose window has four of his panels representing *Youth, Adulthood, Old Age and Death* and a little to the right is the effigy of a dog, placed in the corner between the main building and the

DETAIL OF AN ANGEL WITHIN THE INTERIOR OF THE CHURCH OF ST. MICHAEL AND ALL ANGELS AT LOWFIELD HEATH - PHOTO BY AUTHOR

tower. This latter feature was placed so in order to remember Burges' dog that was killed whilst work was being completed on the church. The remarkable hinges on the main door are also worthy of a close look.

Inside, there is further exquisite carving on the pulpit and font as well as either side of the chancel arch. Here there are two faces represented, one of them blindfolded which refer to a passage from St. John's Gospel. There is further sculptural work on the brackets that support the gallery, this time showing a typical Pre-Raphaelite subject-angels with their musical instruments. The stained glass is good, most of it being by Hemming & Co. Although the church is not so ornate as Burges's churches elsewhere (such as Studley Royal) it is still a very Pre-Raphaelite experience. ***The church is often locked but access is through contact with the church warden.***

THE STRIKING EXTERIOR OF BURGES'S CHURCH AT LOWFIELD HEATH - PHOTO BY AUTHOR

'THE BLIND GIRL' BY JOHN EVERETT MILLAIS - PERMISSION OF BIRMINGHAM MUSEUMS AND ART GALLERY

'OUR ENGLISH COASTS' BY WILLIAM HOLMAN HUNT - PERMISSION OF THE TATE

'BIANCA' BY WILLIAM HOLMAN HUNT - PERMISSION OF WORTHING MUSEUM AND ART GALLERY

DETAIL OF THE ARCHANGEL RAPHAEL FROM THE TILED REREDOS IN CLAPHAM CHURCH - PHOTO BY AUTHOR

'MOONLIT SEA, TURKEY' BY EDWARD LEAR - PERMISSION OF WORTHING MUSEUM AND ART GALLERY

'RYE PORT' BY ALBERT GOODWIN - PERMISSION OF WORTHING MUSEUM AND ART GALLERY

TWO ANGELS WITH HARPS FROM THE STAINED GLASS WINDOW IN THE CHURCH OF THE ANNUNCIATION, BRIGHTON - PHOTO BY AUTHOR

Trail No. 5 Around Cuckfield

Points of Interest

(1) NEWICK-ST. MARY'S CHURCH - nice restored Victorian interior with stained glass in the style of Burne-Jones.****

(2) FLETCHING - CHURCH OF ST. ANDREW AND ST. MARY THE VIRGIN- Good examples of Kempe glass particularly in huge east window ****

(3) MARESFIELD - CHURCH OF ST.BARTHOLOMEW- Powell glass in atmospheric interior.***

(4) FAIRWARP - CHRIST CHURCH - Stunning stained glass in a grand building ***.

(5) LITTLE HORSTED - CHURCH OF ST. MICHAEL AND ALL ANGELS - Late window by Eleanor Fortescue-Brickdale, the Pre-Raphaelite follower ***.

Also: churches at Framfield, Nutley.

STARTING POINT: Newick church is to the south of the village green that lies beside the main A272.

HOW TO GET THERE: the church is tucked away but sign-posted with a car park to the south of the building

FINISHING POINT: Little Horsted church

REFRESHMENTS: Good pubs in Fletching and Newick.

TRANSPORT: Only possible by car.

DURATION: Morning/ afternoon or leisurely full day.

NEWICK CHURCH (1) was the subject of what has been described as a sympathetic restoration, in 1886 by John Oldrid Scott, the second son of Sir Giles Gilbert Scott. The younger man was probably indirectly responsible for much of the decoration in the chancel, with its painted ceiling that uses fleur-de-lis patterning and has a range of differing roof bosses. There are also a number of carved stalls to be seen as well as the exquisite reredos which the church guide book attributes to a Mr. Brown, who was 'a disciple of Sir Edward C. Burne-Jones'. It is unclear whether he was a local

POWELL GLASS AT NEWICK CHURCH - PHOTO BY AUTHOR

man responding to the inspiration of Burne-Jones but the reredos is certainly a fine object. The guide also suggests that one of the windows was designed by Burne-Jones but this is almost certainly not the case. The window in question shows *The Virgin and Infant Christ* and is in the choir aisle to the left of the chancel and does contain a very good border. Next to it is the predominately blue window illustrating the 150th. Psalm with its six angels carrying their instruments, which undoubtedly has an initial similarity to Burne-Jones' work although on closer examination, the expressions on the faces are unlikely to be by his hand. In the nave is a version of *The Light of the World* which is of interest (but very different to Holman Hunt's interpretation)and in the north aisle a well balanced group ensemble piece showing *Emmanuel, St. Stephen, St. John and the Holy Innocents* from 1903. All the glass at Newick is by Powell with the exception of one window in the north aisle that was produced by the company of Cox & Barnard. The interior gives a good idea of how the Victorians attempted to recreate the medieval church and has work that was obviously inspired by the whole Pre-Raphaelite ethos without having any direct connections to the movement. **The church is open most days.**

The next stop is at (2) FLETCHING CHURCH which is reached by taking the A272 west and turning left at Piltdown. The church steeple can be seen from quite a distance and is a local landmark. The thirteenth century east window was restored in 1880 and contains pleasing Kempe glass illustrating *The Adoration* across its three lights. His wheatsheaf motif is present and the window commemorates a Rev. Attenborough, who is also remembered by the rather Pre-Raphaelite angel on his grave adjacent to the path leading to the porch. There is more modest Kempe glass in the chancel but his window in the south transept is more remarkable (1894). This has an unusual balance of colour which certainly helps to differentiate between the earthly and celestial subject matter. On a nice sunny day, it is easy to appreciate the fine detailing in Kempe's work which is one of the reasons he is commonly associated with the Pre-Raphaelites. *The church is open most days.*

SCULPTURE IN THE CHURCHYARD AT FLETCHING - PHOTO BY AUTHOR

The next definite stop is Maresfield but a pause can be made at Nutley church which contains Powell glass in the north aisle dating from 1907-23.

Maresfield is sign-posted from the A22 a little to the north-east of Uckfield. ST. BARTHOLOMEW'S CHURCH (3) was also restored by the Victorians with the transepts and chancel being the work once again of J. Oldrid Scott, whose abilities were previously seen at Newick. Here, he seems to have really gone to town, reusing the old chancel arch in his north transept and moving the old east window to the south transept. The glass in his replacement east window illustrates scenes from the *Passion and Deposition*. Although the angels outside the main scenes appear inferior, some of the larger figures show a Burne-Jones influence and are depicted with considerable emotion. Although the north transept window is poor, the one opposite to the south is interesting with its colourful quarried glass, designed as it was by the daughter of John Villiiers Shelley of Maresfield Place, to whom it is commemorated. The highlight of the interior is to be found in the first window on the north side of the chancel. This shows *St. Peter and St. Paul* with smaller predella scenes below. Its use of naturalism and very deep colours are typical of the high quality of much later Powell glass where the legacy of Burne-Jones' time with the company, is only too apparent. *The church may be locked but access is available through one of the church wardens.*

A couple of miles to the north alongside the B2026, and on the fringes of the Ashdown Forest stands the rather grand (4) CHRIST CHURCH at Fairwarp. Dating from 1881 and a rare example of the work of the architect, Rhode Hawkins it was significantly extended in the 1930's when a polygonal apse was added to its east end. It is within this that there are four unexpectedly deep coloured windows, that initially appear more modern than they in fact are. The glass originally formed the main east window of the unaltered building and therefore predates its present location by at least forty years. The current setting certainly gives the windows an unusual appearance but the designs themselves are particularly bold and innovative for their time. There are a number of other good windows in the church some of which have the characteristics of the Powell workshop, but they pale in comparison to the four windows in the chancel. Not surprisingly they were designed by Henry Holiday in 1885 during his heyday at Powell & Sons and perhaps the main inspiration for them lies in the work that Burne-Jones was producing at about that time. Before leaving a visit should be made to the churchyard where there are some impressive monuments to the Eckstein family. *The church may be locked, in which case access can be arranged through one of the church wardens listed on the notice board in the porch.*

The next stop in this itinerary is Little Horsted to the south of Uckfield, but on the way a pause can be taken at the CHURCH OF ST. THOMAS BECKET at Framfield. *This is found by taking the A272 west and then following signs on the right hand side to the village.* There is a reredos by J.D. Sedding, an architect, who was involved with the Arts and Crafts Exhibition Society and a man who was also strongly influenced by Ruskin. In addition, the church also contains two windows hidden either side of the sanctuary and dating from the turn of the last century, which in their sepia tones have qualities associated with Pre-Raphaelite ideals. They are from the workshops of Powell & Sons. *The church is open most days.*

The (5) CHURCH OF ST. MICHAEL AND ALL ANGELS at Little Horsted is *beside the main A26 road to Lewes about a couple of miles outside Uckfield.* It was

Sir Gilbert Scott who restored this building in 1863, financed by the wealthy Barchard family who at the time lived nearby at Horsted Place. Inside, there are impressive carvings on the octagonal font and pulpit but it is the east window that particularly merits attention. This *Crucifixion* has strange elongated figures and a predominance of blue and green colours as well as a number of birds including a robin and a thrush. The figures have serene facial expressions and overall the effect on the viewer is one of surprise at its originality. The window is in fact a late work (1932) by Eleanor Fortescue-Brickdale, a Pre-Raphaelite follower. Although it serves to show how the style of her work did change over time, the difference between this window and others she designed in this church, and the conventional Victorian work evident, is still amazing. She was also responsible for the windows showing *St. Francis* and the *Madonna and Child* as well as the two lancets depicting the archangels *Michael and Gabriel*. These figures are also elongated in a manner not dissimilar to the early paintings of Rossetti and show her bird motif as well. *The church is open regularly.*

DETAIL OF THE MAIN EAST WINDOW AT LITTLE HORSTED - PHOTO BY AUTHOR

Trail No. 6 By the seaside: Eastbourne

Points of Interest

(1) **BEACHY HEAD**

Swinburne wrote evocative poetry whilst viewing this landscape and it was used by Ford Madox Brown as the background to one of his paintings

EASTBOURNE

(2) **ALL SAINTS' HOSPITAL AND CHAPEL**

Where Maria Rossetti spent time in convalescence and was a member of 'The Sisters of the Poor' community***

(3) **CHURCH OF ST. SAVIOUR AND ST. PETER**

Clayton & Bell mosiacs, Powell glass and a carved wooden altar by George Jack, a pupil of William Morris ****.

(4) **CHURCH OF ST. ANDREW**

Morris stained glass ***.

Also: TOWNER ART GALLERY

STARTING POINT: Beachy Head car park, or if only doing the town trail, All Saints hospital at Meads, on the western side of Eastbourne adjacent to the seafront.

HOW TO GET THERE CAR: From the A259 take the sign-posted Beachy Head road on the western side of Eastbourne. After seeing the cliffs follow the road into the town marked 'seafront', After a series of near hairpin bends you arrive at the front proper and the hospital is on the left after a few yards.

PUBLIC TRANSPORT/ ON FOOT: the Guide Friday bus stops at Beachy Head as do some other buses. There are also a number of footpaths to the cliffs.

FINISHING POINT: Wish Road, Eastbourne

REFRESHMENTS: Many outlets in the town

TRANSPORT: CAR/PUBLIC TRANSPORT/ ON FOOT.

DURATION: Morning /afternoon or leisurely full day

BEACHY HEAD (1) is where the South Downs reaches the sea. At over 500 feet above sea level, these chalk cliffs are a famous landmark on the Sussex coast, not always for the right reasons(it is frequently used as a means of suicide). The red and white granite lighthouse was built in 1902, a number of years after Ford Madox Brown used the landscape as the background to his work, *The Body of Harold brought before William the Conqueror*. This picture was completed as a submission to the competition of 1844 for fresco designs in the new Houses of Parliament. Brown did not win but it is characteristic of him to use a recognisable place in a manner totally 'Pre-Raphaelite'(he also used Sompting church in another painting). The area was also the inspiration for a poet closely associated with the movement, Algernon Swinburne. In 1886 he wrote his poem To A Seamew whilst at Beachy Head. The sounds of the many seagulls echo in his work:

> *Thy cry from windward clanging*
> *Makes all the cliffs rejoice;*
> *Though storm clothe seas with sorrow,*
> *Thy call salutes the morrow'*

Now head down to the Meads district of Eastbourne (see directions above). Although it may look much older, (2) ALL SAINTS HOSPITAL is of the Gothic Revival style and was only completed in 1869. The instigator for its creation, was Harriet Brownlow Byron who as Mother Harriet, raised funds so that people could convalesce by the seaside after a major illness. The hospital was a satellite of the community known as the All Saints' Sisters of the Poor in London.

The architect was Henry Woodyer who also designed the impressive chapel, which was added when the earlier integral chapel was found to be unsatisfactory. It has been incorrectly attributed to William Butterfield who was responsible for the building of All Saints' church in Margaret Street, London, where Mother Harriet attended in her earlier days.

ALL SAINTS HOSPITAL IN EASTBOURNE - PHOTO BY AUTHOR

It was also the community that Maria Rossetti joined on the 21st. February 1860 when she felt the need to commit herself to greater religious and charitable work. It was about this time that she relinquished hopes of ever marrying and devoted herself increasingly to a life of faith. Maria herself convalesced at the Home (as it was originally called) in late 1873 after contracting erysipelas, an infection of the skin that was considered a dangerous disease at the time.

The chapel was blessed in 1874, the same year that Christina and her mother stayed at Southsea House on Marine Parade in the town, from where she wrote to Gabriel-

'Our sitting-room here reminds me of beloved Kelmscott, though I fear you would draw the line at its wallpaper'.

Her mother had been unwell and Christina also wrote that

'She (mother) goes out for her little walks, her little sits, her church, and I hope is on the mend for this long while to come'.

The trail will pass the site of this boarding house. Two years later, Christina and her mother spent the summer in Eastbourne to be near Maria who was again in All Saints. This was partly to escape their Euston Square home where William Rossetti and his wife Lucy (Madox Brown's daughter) were resident. There had been some frictions between Christina and Lucy. However Maria's health suddenly declined and Christina wrote to Lucy telling her that

'our trial here has been and still continues to be poor Maria's very grave indisposition.'

She had cancer and upon her return to London in November sadly died.

The chapel remains a lofty and splendidly decorated space. Just outside the chapel door is an old photograph of the Mother Foundress. **The chapel is open most days but access may change when the hospital closes down.**

After taking in the chapel's grandeur, leave the hospital and head into the centre of the town along the seafront road which is also called Grand Parade. Just after you have passed the pier the part of the road known as Marine Parade begins and on your left is where Christina and her mother convalesced at Southsea House (no longer evident). Take the next left into the road known as Seaside and a further left turn will bring you to Pevensey Road. This is now a rather neglected area but where Christina and her mother stayed on another therapeutic visit to the town in July 1880 (they stayed at No.111). On this occasion she wrote to Gabriel commenting on what she may have considered one of his primary interests;

'One very simply dressed lady whom I saw once showed a face that I fancy might have charmed even you by its natural rare beauty; but I have scarcely noticed one other at all exceptional, if even one.'

She continues to paint a somewhat negative view of Eastbourne later in the same letter -

'The horrors of this place would certainly overwhelm you, - its idlers, brass bands, nigger minstrels of British breed, and other attractions; but I, more frivolous, am in a degree amused.'

Head into the town centre along Seaside, cross over a roundabout and find St. Saviour's church on the left.

The (3) CHURCH OF ST. SAVIOUR was founded in 1867 and its present dedication with St. Peter is due to the demolition of the nearby church of that name in the 1970's. It is certainly one of the town's most graceful buildings with a history associated with the Oxford Movement, something so allied to early Pre-Raphaelite concerns. It was designed by George Edmund Street and contains a wealth of Victorian

PART OF THE DECORATIVE SCHEME BY CLAYTON & BELL IN ST. SAVIOURS CHURCH IN EASTBOURNE - PHOTO BY AUTHOR

decoration. The floor tiling is of interest as are the mosaics by Clayton & Bell in both the nave and in the arcades within the sanctuary. There is further work by Clayton & Bell in the more unusual form of a mural over the chancel arch. The font was designed by Street and the only disappointment in the interior is the lack of original glass caused by bombing during the last war. There is still however windows by Clayton & Bell in the clerestory and the south aisle. Be sure not to miss the chapel of the Blessed Sacrament attached to this aisle, where there are further wonderful Clayton & Bell lancets on the west wall. Directly opposite on the north side of the church is an altar by George Jack, a designer of furniture for Morris & Co. Made of oak it shows the Entombment of Christ and is probably here as a result of Jack being in the employ of Street at the time. **The church is open regularly.**

A trip through the back streets of the town with their impressive Victorian buildings will bring you to the (4) CHURCH OF ST. ANDREW **in Wish Road.** This rather unprepossessing building houses the only Morris glass now in the town. (Prior to the last war there were two panels in the chapel of St. Cyprian's school in Summerdown Road where there are a couple of blue heritage plaques marking the location of this building for those interested. These depicted *Christ blessing the Children* with *Women bringing Children* but both were lost through bombing. The window at Wadhurst church (see Trail No.9) has the same designs and therefore gives some idea of how the window appeared.)

The three large lights at St. Andrew's justly dominate the interior where there is also minor, more modern glass. On the left is the *Virgin and Child* in a design by Henry Dearle and the same artist is responsible for the middle light showing the Ascension.

The right-hand panel shows the *Crucifixion* and this is an adapted design from the original by Burne-Jones. All the windows date from 1913 and although clearly not in the top league of Morris glass, transform this otherwise rather plain interior. **The church is occasionally locked but access can be made at times of services and meetings or through the caretaker.**

ALSO:
THE TOWNER ART GALLERY
Located close to the Old Town, the gallery is housed in a former manor house. Its collection has a number of Pre-Raphaelite inspired works although it is wise to check if these are on display. There are paintings by Alma Tadema and Albert Goodwin as well as *On the River Cuckmere* by Leopold Rivers - a fine landscape in a late Millais mode.

THE MORRIS & CO WINDOW IN ST. ANDREWS CHURCH EASTBOURNE - PHOTO BY AUTHOR

Trail No. 7 The Levels, the Weald and Beyond

Points of Interest

(1)   PEVENSEY CASTLE - a Rossetti favourite

(2)   PEVENSEY CHURCH - Atmospheric interior with Morris inspired stained glass***

(3)   HERSTMONCEUX VILLAGE AND CHURCH - More Morris inspired glass and a likely design source for the Firm's Sussex chair.***

(4)   DALLINGTON CHURCH - Very late glass by Duncan W Dearle***

(5)   WARBLETON CHURCH - Kempe glass in a fine setting***

(6)   EAST HOATHLY CHURCH - Powell windows and mosaics in an undiscovered gem****

(7)   CHIDDINGLY CHURCH - More Powell glass**

(8)   SELMESTON CHURCH - More Kempe glass**

(9)   BERWICK CHURCH - Opportunity to see Victorian glass and Bloomsbury murals side by side***

STARTING POINT: Car park at Pevensey Castle

HOW TO GET THERE: Located close to the junction of A259 and A27 to the north-east of Eastbourne

FINISHING POINT: Berwick near Alfriston

REFRESHMENTS: Good pubs at Pevensey, Chiddingly and Berwick

TRANSPORT: Car essential

DURATION: Full day

Before commencing this trail a stop off can be made at Pevensey Bay, a small coastal village a mile or so to the south of the starting point.

It was here that Val Prinsep had a studio from about 1900 until his death in 1904. It was his earlier friendship with Rossetti that first inclined him towards the Pre-Raphaelite style of painting and he was one of the eight artists who contributed to the decoration of the new hall of the Union Society at Oxford in 1858. He also visited Italy on one occasion in the company of Burne-Jones. His later work was much broader in style as can be seen in his Goose Girl of 1900 (Walker Gallery, Liverpool) a work largely completed locally. It is thought that he purchased land that included two of the Martello Towers on the seafront (no's 60 and 61) and may have used one as a residence. He continued to run a large prestigious home at Holland Park in London. There is a Val Prinseps Road on the western side of the village as well as a Rosetti Road (spelt in error) although there is no clear evidence that Rossetti ever visited (he of course died in 1882). There is also a Leyland Road, which is undoubtedly named after Prinsep's wife Florence Leyland, the daughter of Frederick Leyland, industrialist and regular patron of the Pre-Raphaelites.

Two years before his death Dante Gabriel Rossetti mentions (1) PEVENSEY CASTLE in one of his family letters. He describes it as *'a beautiful ruin'* and although it never appears in any of his pictures, it would not have been a surprise to see it so. In his time, the castle was overgrown with ivy and probably much more 'romantic' than its current appearance. However, there is little doubt that its restoration, financed by English Heritage will help preserve it for years to come. **The castle is open most days.**

Just to the east of the castle is the (2) CHURCH OF ST. NICOLAS. It was much restored in the 1870's when the tower was increased in height. Inside to the right, is a small lancet window showing the saint to which the church is dedicated. There is an accompanying window in the opposite corner, this time depicting *St. Wilfrid*. Of more interest though, are the two windows in the south aisle, one a *Resurrection* with the inscription, 'He is not here He is risen', the other an *Annunciation*. These were designed by A. L. Moore and show Morris like qualities which make them very satisfying in their composition. The main east window is also worthy of individual mention, with its three predella scenes below the main subject of *Christ in Majesty* across all three lights. It has the same date of 1875 as that of the chancel restoration and was produced by Clayton & Bell. **The church is open most days.**

Upon leaving the castle car park turn left to continue in an eastwards direction around the perimeter of the castle. After passing much of the village of Westham look for a turning on the right called Peelings Lane and follow this to a crossroads where you should go right. You will now travel through the village of Hankham and you should follow signs to Rickney for the road that traverses the area known as the Pevensey Levels. Avoid a left turn signposted Hailsham to continue on to the hamlet of Rickney. Now take the road left towards Hailsham but then almost immediately go right where a sign says Herstmonceux.

You will now find yourself on a narrow bendy road crossing the Levels where the low horizon (weather permitting) allows views of the distant South Downs and also of Turneresque weather formations.

When you regain more familiar Sussex countryside continue right following signs showing (3)HERSTMONCEUX CHURCH. Upon arrival at this surprisingly large church have a look around its interesting churchyard with great views, only marginally spoiled by the detritus of the adjacent farm.

Inside there is the rather gaudy Powell east window of 1855 which commemorates

A VIEW ACROSS THE PEVENSEY LEVELS - PHOTO BY AUTHOR

Julius Charles Hare who was rector for 23 years. In addition he was Archdeacon of Lewes for 14 years and on one occasion was visited by Thomas Carlyle. Of much greater beauty is the window that commemorates the Rev. Robert Wild on the south side of the chancel. This dates from 1913 and shows the *Virgin Mary and St. John* and appears distinctly Morris inspired being designed by William Glasby who was a glass-painter for both Morris & Co and Powell before becoming a designer in his own right. After this unexpected delight you may wish to view other aspects of the church which has much Victorian restoration including the bearable dormer windows. There is also a small sculpture of a child which the guide book to the church attributes to a French artist, Jean Goujon. Opposite the South window there is a monument to Georgina, the wife of a local landowner (1886) which just about qualifies to be Pre-Raphaelite in the widest use of the phrase. **The church is open regularly.**

Before you leave this area, you might like to ponder that this idyllic location maybe where a Morris chair originated from. This adjustable-back chair was produced by Morris, Marshall, Faulkner & Co. from 1866 to a design by Philip Webb. However, it was Warington Taylor (the firm's manager)who sketched a model for this chair, probably having seen it in the workshop of Ephraim Colman, a carpenter in the village. Webb no doubt modified it to some degree and later it was mass produced, even receiving a mention in the lyrics of a Bing Crosby song of 1922.

Leaving along the same road, take the first right turn towards the main part of Herstmonceux. Continue right along the A271 until Windmill Hill and turn left sign-posted to Bodle Street Green. By following subsequent signs the village of Dallington will be reached where the church is found on the right hand side.

The present (4) CHURCH OF ST. GILES dates mainly from around 1864 when

A DETAIL OF THE VERY PRE - RAPHAELITE STYLED GLASS THAT ADORNS THE INTERIOR OF THE CHURCH OF ST. GILES AT DALLINGTON - PHOTO BY AUTHOR

the old church was demolished with the exception of the tower and steeple. Inside, there is Victorian glass in the main east window and glass described in the guide book as being '*in the Kempe tradition*' on the south side of the chancel.

Of more interest however, are the two windows opposite one another in the nave. The one on the south, in memory of Caroline Tatham, presumably dates from the second decade of the last century and is Morris influenced being designed by William Glasby. The window opposite presents more difficulties in regard to its origin. These two lights also commemorate members of the Tatham family, and may well have a more direct connection to Morris despite their probable date of 1950. The window shows *The Calling of St. John* and was most likely designed by Duncan W. Dearle who was the son of J.H. Dearle and who bought the stained glass section of Morris & Co. in 1940. His style bears some comparisons with earlier Morris work although the colours used appear less subtle. **The church is open regularly.**

Continue northwards to join the B2096 and turn left towards Heathfield but before arriving there take the minor road on the left hand side to Warbleton. The (5) CHURCH OF ST. MARY has a remarkable 'squire's pew' that is high over the north aisle of the nave, supported by very substantial posts. This and the sculpture of Sir John Lade by Rysbrack are perhaps the building's most obvious claims to fame but there is also a good window by Kempe. This is the west window and dates from the 1880's, when a gallery was removed as it obstructed the view of the new window. The design has a great sense of movement although parishioners of the time must have been concerned over the loss of light to the interior as it replaced clear glass. Also of interest is the red and gold screen on the wall to the right hand side of the entrance that dates from a similar time when the church was becoming more richly decorated. It now appears to be out of favour. *The church is open most days.*

After returning to your car continue northwards taking the first left down Furnace Lane and later left again along Nettlesworth Lane into Vines Cross. This route across the Sussex Weald continues right towards Horam then left sign-posted Hailsham to join the A267. Take a right towards Cross-in-Hand and look for a minor road on the left sign-posted to Waldron and also called Furnace Lane. After this keep following the signs towards the next destination, East Hoathly. On arrival you will soon see a road to the Parish Church going right.

Before entering (6) EAST HOATHLY CHURCH have a look at the impressive family grave of the Ricketts who lived in nearby Barham House. Its four angels have a style associated with Pre-Raphaelite sculpture

PART OF THE EXTENSIVE MURALS AT EAST HOATHLY CHURCH - PHOTO COURTESY OF THE RECTOR

and are very pleasing. Upon entering the church the eye is drawn to the mosaics behind the altar on the east wall. These have a quite clear Pre-Raphaelite appearance and were designed by Powells and installed in 1885. It may be that they were not designed specifically for this location but may have been selected from a catalogue of the firm's designs by the Borrodaile children in order to honour their parents. Nevertheless the mosaics harmonise well with their surroundings and convince as a whole piece. The orangey brown tiles below showing foliage are particularly Morris like. The window above was commissioned

THE STAINED GLASS BY POWELLS AT CHIDDINGLY CHURCH - PHOTO BY AUTHOR

by the same Ricketts family as the monument just seen in the graveyard. It dates from 1883 and was designed by the Lancaster firm of Shrigley & Hunt. Their chief designer at this time was Carl Almquist who had trained under the direction of Henry Holiday. His own designs were inspired by Holiday, although perhaps here, they pale beside the exuberant mosaics. Other windows of note include one in the south wall of the nave, in memory of Caroline Sarah Clements which together with the window adjacent is richly decorative and also designed by Shrigley & Hunt. Another window in remembrance of Sophia Clements in the north wall, is worthy of note although the glass showing *The Crucifixion* in the west window surpasses this. This satisfying composition across three lights with its convincing perspective is the best in the building and once again comes from the company of Shrigley & Hunt. There is much fine ironwork and carving to be admired also. ***The church is open regularly.***

East Hoathly lays claim to being a possible source for the Morris produced range of 'Sussex' chairs. Whilst there does not appear to be any definite evidence for this claim (although Ernest Jones, a past headmaster in the village, is said to have drawn a design for a similar chair) there may well be some truth in the story. The chairs were all based on traditional country styles and adapted by various members of the firm. There are several of these rush-seated ebonised chairs in the kitchen corridor at Standen.

Retrace your steps and go down one of the roads to Chiddingly and you will shortly notice the tower of the church which is a distinctive local landmark. Naturally enough, the Jefferay monument of 1612 will effortlessly grab your attention after coming through the porch door of (7) CHIDDINGLY CHURCH. There is not much competition from a poor east window but the gem of this church is to be found in the north east corner of the nave close to the font. This window of deep hues and delicate leaves was made by Powells and depicts *St. John the Baptist* and *St. John the Evangelist* and dates from 1876. As can be seen from the inscription it commemorates a local landowner who lived at Uckfield. The facial features are very expressive and calming. ***The church is open most days.***

To continue turn back and opposite the Six Bells go left in the direction of Golden Cross. Turn left on the busy A22 and then almost immediate right towards Chalvington and then follow three signs to Selmeston. The undedicated (8) SELMESTON CHURCH was also restored in Victorian times but perhaps more sympathetically than others and has some nice watercolours inside that show the church prior to this. Amongst some bright inferior windows is a good Kempe *'Annunciation'* in the north aisle where the lilies shown have a naturalistic quality similar to the early work of Rossetti. The Kempe signatory wheatsheaf can also be seen. Before leaving do not miss the book rest supported by two angels in the chancel and the pleasing woodcarving on the pews. ***The church is open most days.***

To conclude this trail drive along the A27 in the direction of Eastbourne until Berwick is sign-posted to the right. The (9) CHURCH OF ST. MICHAEL AND ALL ANGELS is to be found right at the back of the village and is a place of homage for the 'Bloomsberries'. When you first enter the church you may be surprised at how the murals completed by Vanessa Bell, Duncan Grant and Quentin Bell give the interior a quite unique ambience. The fact that they are here at all is the result of one man's endeavour, Bishop Bell, the Bishop of Chichester from 1929 to 1957, who believed in close ties between the worlds of church and art. The murals were worked on at nearby Charleston (they are on plasterboard) and completed in 1943. They rather dwarf the remaining panels of stained glass (some were lost in the war), but which is of good quality. The glass forms part of the Victorian 'restoration' of the church which effectively transformed it from a near ruin.

The main east window shows the *Ascension* and is in memory of Edward Boys Ellman, the man responsible for much of the Victorian rebuilding. Its distinctive angels and good use of space suggest a Morris influence and the window is by Powell & Sons (1908) who produced all the windows in this church. There are also the figures of three saints in the chancel as well as another Ellman family window in the south aisle, depicting Dorcas and Phoebe. The windows are not in the premier league but undoubtedly deserve a mention, which they do not receive in the church guide.

The church is open most days.

Trail No. 8 Lewes and Rottingdean

Points of Interest

LEWES

(1) CHURCH OF ST. MICHAEL - windows designed by Henry Holiday in a moody interior****

(2) CHURCH OF ST. JOHN - Kempe windows and an imposter!**

(3) KINGSTON CHURCH - Morris inspired glass**

(4) DENTON CHURCH - Kempe window**

(5) SEAFORD TOWN AND CHURCH - where Christina Rossetti visited, the site of a Morris window and Heaton, Butler and Bayne glass***

(6) ROTTINGDEAN VILLAGE AND CHURCH - the location of the seaside retreat of Burne-Jones, a museum with a room devoted to him and a church with stunning late glass*****

(7) ROEDEAN SCHOOL

(8) OVINGDEAN VILLAGE AND CHURCH - birthplace of Charles Kempe and where the church contains a number of his creations****

(9) FALMER - scenes associated with Morris.

Also: BARCOMBE CHURCH - Kempe windows***

STARTING POINT: St. Michaels Church in the High Street, Lewes.

HOW TO GET THERE: Lewes is about nine miles to the east of Brighton just off the main A27 Brighton to Eastbourne road.

PUBLIC TRANSPORT: There are regular buses to the town, many pass by the church which is located west of the distinctive Law Courts on the same side of the road. Once the tour leaves the town it is possible to use bus routes but these can be infrequent and difficult to use.

CAR: the High Street is the main through-fare for the town.

FINISHING POINT: Lewes (circular)

REFRESHMENTS: many shops, pubs in Lewes and Seaford as well as teashops at Rottingdean. Pubs at Kingston and Denton.

DURATION: Full day

The outside appearance of the (1) CHURCH OF ST. MICHAEL is a little unusual, due principally to its round tower curiously covered in pebbledash. Once inside however, this and the busy traffic are quickly forgotten as the eye adjusts to what is an exceptional interior. It was Edgar Herman Cross who made extensive changes to the church between1877-1890 resulting in much of its present appearance. So we see a number of windows by Powells and in particular the work of Henry Holiday. It was Holiday who took over from Burne-Jones at Powells when he left to join Morris. Despite the main east window being replaced by more modern work there is still a number of examples of his best work. Some of the windows appear bleached (caused by faulty manufacture)and it was this that necessitated the removal of the east window. The south aisle is impressive with three windows having large figures with grisaille or coloured predellas below and quatrefoils above. The east window of the aisle has two lights of biblical scenes with astonishing bright red haloes around the heads of the figures. The window opposite in the north aisle is almost as good depicting as it does an *Annunciation* and the *Adoration of Christ*. Aside from the marvellous glass be sure to see the murals in the chancel showing angels, the wooden screen to the chapel and the decorated organ. **The church is open regularly.**

When ready to leave, walk or drive to the (2) CHURCH OF ST. JOHN THE BAPTIST *to the south of the town in Southover High Street.*

This interior of this church will probably be a disappointment after St. Michaels and certainly the quality of the glass is not so uniformly good. Nevertheless there are compensations. You can see five Kempe windows and one by Herbert Bryans all with life size saint figures on the north wall as well as a further Kempe window of 1883 in the south aisle(with the wheatsheaf trademark shown on a shield). Of curiosity value is the western most window in the south aisle. The church guide describes this as Morris work and indeed it is signed William Morris & Co. (Westminster) with a date on the inscription of 1935. However this glass is definitely not genuine Morris, but a firm attempting to trade off his reputation. In fact its appearance has little connection to the real thing, a fact that will be confirmed by the windows to be seen later in this trail. *The church is open regularly.*

If a car is being used you should now make your way out of Lewes going in a westerly direction along Southover High Street, turning to the left by The Swan pub. This is the road to Kingston, going over the bypass and where later you should follow signs to the village and then signs to the church.

The (3) CHURCH OF ST. PANCRAS had a very thorough 'restoration' in 1874 and its interior is rather bare and unpromising. Its great redeeming feature is the east

A DETAIL OF THE MAIN EAST WINDOW AT THE CHURCH OF ST. PANCRAS IN KINGSTON NEAR LEWES - PHOTO BY AUTHOR

window as well as two smaller windows-one a virtual abstract design and the other a memorial window to an artist Betty Dora Leney, who died in 1981. Both are outside the remit of this book but the main window is certainly a late flowering of the Pre-Raphaelite style. It shows *Christ in Majesty* (in a design similar to the work of Dearle) in the centre with Mary amongst the crowd to the right. On the left-hand side there is a bearded figure who curiously has a passing resemblance to Burne-Jones! Because of the composition the colours of the window are lighter in the top half (to emphasise the celestial) with earthier greens and reds below. The window was designed by Powell & Sons in 1908. *The church is open most days.*

Leave the village by the same road of arrival but now turn right at the Lewes road. At Newhaven go over the harbour bridge on the A259 to see Denton and Seaford (sign-posted Eastbourne) or if you are time limited, follow the same road in the opposite direction to Rottingdean (sign-posted Brighton). Follow the signposts to Denton that appear soon after leaving the port, the church is to be found on an incline amongst modern development.

The (4) CHURCH OF ST. LEONARD was the subject of two 'restorations' in 1865 and 1901. There is little stained glass except the main east window which is by Kempe and dated 1895. It shows the *Adoration* over its four lights with angels over the central scene and predella scenes below with circular borders. This is superior work for the date with Pre-Raphaelite influences evident but within Kempe's own unique interpretation. The largish church retains some atmosphere despite its radically altered environment, nestled as it is amidst a sea of bungalows. *The church is open regularly.*

Continue along the A259 to the town of Seaford. The road passes Bishopstone which is on the left just outside the town. Bishopstone House in the village was for a number of years owned by Denis Mackail, the grandson of Burne-Jones who became an author.

Seaford is where Christina Rossetti stayed in July 1879 for a period of convalescence. She stayed at a boarding house at 2, Gladstone Villas which sadly has been demolished, the post office now occupies the site. She wrote to both Gabriel and William Morris whilst in the town.

Many years later, some Morris glass was installed in the chapel of the Kingsmead preparatory school for boys in Belgrave Road. This showed *Christ Preaching from the Ship* and was a design of Henry Dearle's across three lights. It dates from 1927-29. Alas, it is now difficult to see as the school closed and the Edwardian building is now a nursing home. Access to the now dilapidated chapel is discouraged and local history groups are said to be concerned for its survival. However, as a small compensation there are some interesting photos of the school taken in the period 1911-20 in the lobby of the present building.

The (5) PARISH CHURCH OF ST. LEONARD is large as befits the main ecclesiastical building of a former cinque port. Its main delights in the stained glass field are windows by Kempe and by Heaton, Butler and Bayne. The former are on the south wall of the nave and show *St. Leonard*(the patron saint of the church), *St. Wilfrid* and *St. Pancras the Martyr,* with his sword, palm and book. It is good for its late date of 1901. Better still, are the two windows by Heaton, Butler and Bayne which are to be found in the Chapel of the Holy Spirit. These depict the allegorical figures of *Charity* and *Sacrifice* and date from the twenties, a long time after the firm's association with Henry Holiday, although his influence and that of Morris and Burne-Jones is still apparent. *The church is open most weekday mornings.*

Now head back along the A259 past Newhaven and Peacehaven until you arrive

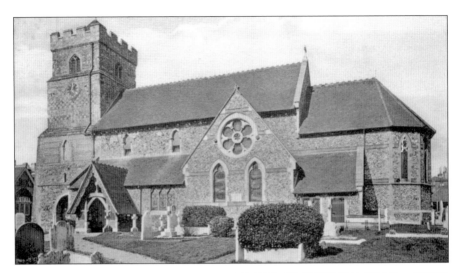

THE PARISH CHURCH OF ST. LEONARD SEAFORD IN VICTORIAN TIMES - PHOTO COURTESY OF STEVE BENZ

at the village of (6) ROTTINGDEAN. *As you head up the High Street from the south, the house that Burne-Jones used as a seaside retreat from 1880-1898 is on the left, facing the church and the village green.* PROSPECT HOUSE (now called Cottage) has a blue heritage sign outside and it was this house that Georgiana first saw for sale. Nine years later in 1889, Burne-Jones was able to acquire the adjacent property, Aubrey Cottage and he then renamed the two properties, North End House.

THE TWO PROPERTIES ON THE LEFT MADE UP THE FORMER HOME OF BURNE - JONES AT ROTTINGDEAN - PHOTO BY AUTHOR

Rather confusingly, the house on the other side of Aubrey Cottage is now named North End House but was previously called Gothic House. The unusual exterior of Aubrey Cottage no doubt owes much to W.A.S. Benson, who planned the joining together of the two properties. The new choice of name relates to the address of their London home which the family kept on throughout this period. It was here in Rottingdean that the young Rudyard Kipling came to visit his aunt and uncle and where Burne-Jones spent many a happy time away from the bustle of Fulham. The house was later lived in by the author, Enid Bagnold.

A walk across the green passes the house (The Elms) where Kipling lived prior to Batemans and brings you to the CHURCH OF ST. MARGARET. In the churchyard, are the final resting places of Ned and Georgiana as well as their grand-daughter Angela Thirkell, whose book *Three Houses* describes life at North End House, where Burne-Jones was very much the doting granddad. Their ashes lie by the south-west corner of the building indicated by stone tablets for Ned and Georgiana and by a wooden 'bedstead' board for Angela. In addition, the grave of Burne-Jones' friend Cormell Price lies in the churchyard, a man who was also Kipling's old headmaster.

The interior of the church is probably the best example in the whole county of Burne-Jones' stained glass and is undoubtedly a visual feast. The sheer power of his late work, striking in its bold colours, is breathtaking.

Much of what one sees today is the work of Sir George Gilbert Scott, whose 'restoration' of 1856 included the building of the south aisle as well as the east lancet windows which house some of the Morris & Co. glass. Commencing with this window

DETAIL FROM THE ST. MARGARET WINDOW AT ROTTINGDEAN CHURCH DESIGNED BY BURNE-JONES - PHOTO BY AUTHOR

I will describe the Firm's glass, the designs being all by Burne-Jones with the exception of two panels by Henry Dearle.

The three lancets depict, from left to right, *St. Gabriel* with the *Annunciation* below, *St. Michael* with him *Slaying the dragon* underneath and *St. Raphael* with a panel showing a *Guardian angel leading a soul* below. The Latin inscription tells us that the windows commemorate the marriage of Burne-Jones' daughter, Margaret (to J. W. Mackail, a later biographer of Morris) in 1888. They were a personal gift from a loving father and were installed five years later. The two lancets nearby on the north and south walls of the chancel, show *St. Margaret* and *St. Mary the Virgin* respectively. The former was presented to the church by Margaret Burne-Jones(she shares the name of the saint to whom the church is dedicated) and the latter commemorates the wife of the Rev. Arthur Thomas who was the vicar at the time of the windows' installation in 1894. A little further down the chancel and beneath the tower are two further exquisite windows on either side. These two windows date from 1897 and are in memory of the vicar himself. They are both superb examples of the mature style of Burne-Jones. On the north wall, the tall lancet shows *Jacob's Dream* with Jacob asleep at the bottom of a composition of eight angels. It has faint echoes of his *Golden Stairs* painting to be seen in the Tate. Opposite, is his *Tree of Jesse* of which Burne-Jones said *'I should like more space for that; it is the kind of thing that would look glorious spread over an acre of glass'*. Both windows were personally overseen by him during their making and the designs were not used again at any other location.

Finally, there are the windows on the north wall of the nave. The single lancet shows *St. Martin* in his pink armour, with the subject, *Visiting the Sick* in a roundel below. This dates from 1902 and commemorates Edward Ridsdale, whose daughter married Stanley Baldwin, later Prime Minister and also Burne-Jones' nephew. Nearby are the twin lancets showing (on the left) *St. Veronica* with *Christ bearing the Cross* below and (on the right) St George with his dragon in the panel underneath. These windows, with the two lower panels designed by Henry Dearle, date from 1919 and are in memory of a casualty from the Great War. Whilst they have nothing of the drama of the earlier windows in the church with their luminous blues and ruby tones, they do indicate that the glass produced by Morris & Co. years after the deaths of its founders still has the ability to please. The other Victorian glass in the church mainly by Clayton & Bell, provides another opportunity to compare it with the radical glass designs being produced by Burne-Jones at a similar time. **The church is open most days.**

Before leaving the village, be sure to pop into the local museum which is housed in the former vicarage and called The Grange, which upstairs contains a small room devoted to Burne-Jones. There is a full description of his time at Rottingdean in the chapter describing his life.

The next stop is (7) ROEDEAN SCHOOL, *a distinctive building standing beside the main coast road (A259) a little further on in the direction of Brighton. Access to the chapel is only possible by contacting the school beforehand and if you do not wish to visit you can take the road to Ovingdean to the right at the first roundabout after leaving Rottingdean.*

The main building dates from 1898 and was designed by J. W. Simpson in a free Jacobean style. In the entrance hall is a delightful plaque listing the school's founding benefactors who included G.F. Watts. The chapel, which is our main destination, is a later addition of 1906. The rather sumptuous interior houses a range of stained glass in its two galleries, most of which dates from just after the Great War. The Morris glass is on the north side where it is found in the third and fourth windows from the east end. The former shows (on the left) *Christ as Love* from a Burne-Jones design whilst next door is *St. Michael* spearing the Dragon in a Henry Dearle work. The lunette above has an *Angel with Crown and foliage.* This window dates from 1920, three years later than its neighbour. This shows the allegorical figures of *Valour* and *Fortitude,* both being the designs of Henry Dearle. Its lunette has an *Angel with Scroll* which may well be a Morris design by the man himself, adapted from his ceiling decoration at Jesus College chapel.

Roedean chapel provides an unusual setting for the Company's glass both because of its architecture and also the way it houses a lot of work by companies who were at the time, a little long in the tooth. So there is Kempe & Co. Ltd. glass on the south side and what may well be Powells glass next to Morris. There is also a 1906 window designed by Herbert Bryans in the sanctuary. Some of this is of rather average quality but does provide a useful opportunity to compare late works by long established Victorian companies.

Now retrace your tracks along the busy A259 and take the aforementioned road to the old village of Ovingdean.

The (8) CHURCH OF ST. WULFRUN lies a little to the west of the road and must be one of the most beautiful medieval churches within the immediate vicinity of the city of Brighton. It is named after the seventh century Archbishop of Sens in France. In a particularly interesting churchyard are memorials to William Willett (who invented Summer Time) and to Magnus Volk, the man responsible for the 'Daddy Long Legs' railway that so infused Burne-Jones when it started to run, at a time near the end of his life. There is also the tombstone of Nathaniel Kemp opposite the porch, the father of Charles Eamer Kempe who designed it and whom was buried in the same grave when

THE PAINTED TILE PANEL IN OVINGDEAN CHURCH SHOWING THE ENTOMBMENT OF CHRIST - PHOTO BY AUTHOR

he died in 1907. Kempe was born at nearby Ovingdean Hall (now a school) in 1838.

The church was given a 'restoration' in 1865-7 and this was when Kempe painted the attractive roof panels in the chancel. He also designed the rood over the chancel arch although this was completed later. The family coat of arms hangs on the south wall of the nave. In regard to the windows, five of them bear the wheatsheaf monogram in one form or another. These are in the tower and lady chapel, the two larger windows on the south side of the nave and a smaller faded window on the north wall.

Of greater interest are the painted panels in the chancel that commemorate members of the local Anderson family. The lowest one, immediately behind the altar and surrounded by part of the old carved wooden screen is made of tiles. It shows the *Entombment of Christ* and is very Burne-Jones in style. Above it, either side of the small Norman window are two larger panels on wood showing (on the left) the *Agony in the Garden* and opposite the *Resurrection*. All three panels are clearly from the same hand or company with many similarities and the church guide suggests these are the work of Arthur Saville and Alexander Gibbs. The latter may well be the glass firm of Alexander Gibbs, that continued to operate until 1915, about 23 years after the approximate date these panels were completed. They certainly show a Pre-Raphaelite style which is perhaps not surprising in a church so associated with Charles Kempe. The panels above are much later and were completed by a local artist, Maude E. Bishop. *The church is often locked and access may need to be made through the church wardens.*

To continue the tour, follow the road round to the right in the same direction as before. At a junction go ahead and you will shortly join the Falmer Road (B2123) where you should turn left. Pass through Woodingdean but before coming into Falmer look out for a little parking area by the side of the road.

From this point (9) it is possible to get some idea of the view that William Morris enthused about in 1882, when taking a trap out with his elder daughter, Jenny. They were staying at Prospect Cottage and he wrote *'it is very beautiful when you get on to the brow of the hill above Falmer: a long way off to the right you can see Lewes lying like a box of toys under a great amphitheatre of chalk hills: the whole ride is very pleasant'.* Undoubtedly the view has changed with much development apparent including the University buildings, but one can still appreciate it.

The road shortly joins the A27 which takes you back to Lewes.

ALSO: It is possible whilst in the area to visit the church at Barcombe which lies a couple of miles to the north of the town.

The CHURCH OF ST. MARY has a number of high quality Kempe windows. The best are those in the south aisle that date from the early 1880's and show a Pre-Raphaelite influence.

Trail No. 9 The High Weald

Points of Interest

(1) TICEHURST - CHURCH OF SAINT MARY THE VIRGIN- Stained glass by Christopher Whall, a designer involved with the Arts and Crafts Movement***

(2) WADHURST - CHURCH OF ST. PETER AND ST. PAUL - Morris & Co. stained glass ***

(3) ROTHERFIELD -CHURCH OF ST. DENYS - Important Morris glass ****

(4) BURWASH WEALD - CHURCH OF ST. PHILIP - Morris inspired stained glass ***

(5) BURWASH -BATEMANS, Home of Rudyard Kipling from 1902 to 1936. Has Burne-Jones family connections and memorabilia and paintings by Philip Burne-Jones, Poynter and Whistler. (Tel: 01435 882302).

STARTING POINT: Ticehurst church is south of the village square and main road, behind some shops and cottages and surrounded by its large churchyard.

HOW TO GET THERE: the village is on the B2099 between Wadhurst and Hurst Green.

FINISHING POINT: Batemans house (National Trust).

REFRESHMENTS: there are pubs in all villages and a teashop at Batemans

DURATION: Full day.

This trail commences in Ticehurst close to the border with Kent, but you may wish to do it in an alternative order to take into account the opening times at Batemans (April -Oct. daily except Thurs. and Fri. 11-5).
The (1) CHURCH OF ST. MARY THE VIRGIN is mainly fourteenth century but with three major 'restorations' in 1856, 1879 and 1901. One of its best treasures is the exquisitely carved oak font cover, made of eight panels, dating from the sixteenth century. The main perpendicular east window dates from the first Victorian 'restoration', and has glass dating from the second, probably designed by Margaret Holgate Foster, with the central panel painted for the Paris Exhibition of 1878. There

is further glass of good quality on the south side of the chancel where a window of 1875 shows the figures of *The Virgin* and *St. John* on clear quarries and has a Morris inspiration as well as decent Clayton & Bell glass in the south aisle (dated 1882).

But the main reason for visiting this church is another window in the south aisle, second from the right and dated 1889. This is by Powells but is also an early example of the design work of Christopher Whall. He went on to become an advocate of the Arts and

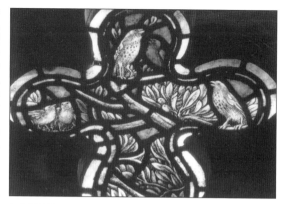

A DETAIL FROM THE STAINED GLASS WINDOW IN TICEHURST CHURCH FROM AN EARLY DESIGN BY CHRISTOPHER WHALL - PHOTO BY THE AUTHOR

Crafts Movement, but early on was inspired by the work of Botticelli and as a result the designs of Burne-Jones. This window incorporates an innovative canopy of foliage around its figures and has a wonderful range of different glasses present. His ability to use nature in his designs is apparent particularly in the lovely use of birds in the quatrefoils above. *The church is open most days. Now head west along the A 2099 to Wadhurst.*

THE WADHURST WINDOW WAS INSTALLED AFTER THE DEATH OF BURNE-JONES AND WAS FIRST USED IN GLASGOW IN 1892 - PHOTO BY AUTHOR

This is a small pretty town, where rather surprisingly, prize-fighting was still a popular pursuit in mid-Victorian times. The large (2) PARISH CHURCH OF ST. PETER AND ST. PAUL is tucked away to the north of the High Street although it is visible for many miles due to its high position above sea level. Uniquely there are over thirty cast iron tomb slabs set into the floor of the church, a sign of Wadhurst's prominence in the Wealden iron industry for nearly three centuries.

You will most likely now be fine tuned to discovering the Pre-Raphaelite interest, which in the case of difficulty is immediately to the left of the entrance. Here in the south-west corner is a window of two lights from a design by Burne-Jones installed in 1899/1900.

To the left is *Christ blessing the Children* whilst *Women bringing Children* is on the right. The scene includes a landscape background with a long scroll beneath that reads *'Suffer little children to come unto me for such is the Kingdom of Heaven'*. Above in the tracery is an angel with a double-pipe and two trefoils show sky.

This basic design had been previously used at nearby Speldhurst in Kent although the design is a little different and was used elsewhere in Sussex, at St. Cyprian's Chapel in Eastbourne in 1912. Unfortunately this was bombed in the last war and it was probably destroyed. Pevsner rightfully notes that the window before us was completed after Morris's death (and after the death of Burne-Jones for that matter) but then goes on to describe it as 'decidedly feeble', something it is difficult to agree with. Whilst the work is comparatively modest and a suitable prelude to what is to come on this trail it is well balanced and understated. ***The church is open most days.***

Whilst being in this area, it is always difficult to resist the urge to visit the Morris

glass centred around Tunbridge Wells, just across the Kent border. This of course remains an option, but the next planned stop will more than compensate for any perceived loss. ***Now head directly down to Rotherfield along the B2100 to one of the most impressive Pre-Raphaelite sights in the county.*** Once again it is found in an ecclesiastical building, the (3) CHURCH OF ST. DENYS. This rather grand church contains many treasures, two particular ones being the finely carved pulpit and the extensive wall paintings. These are worth mentioning early on before one's attention is taken by the main attraction.

This is the large scale fifteenth century Perpendicular east window, with its very beautiful Morris & Co. glass installed in 1878. Its five lights and tracery have as their subject the *Te Deum* with the upper windows showing the archangels, *Raphael, Uriel, Michael* and *Gabriel.* Below them is a heavenly choir with angels holding a variety

THE FIGURE OF ST. BARNABAS AT ROTHERFIELD DESIGNED BY WILLIAM MORRIS - PHOTO BY AUTHOR

of instruments including dulcimers, violins, harps and horns. Further down are the larger figures of *Christ* (holding the world as an orb in his hand) with seraphims and cherubins on either side. In turn, on the middle tier surrounding the *Virgin Mary*, are the saints *Peter* (with the key) and *Paul* (with the sword of the Spirit). Outside of these two, the prophets *Samuel* (vial of oil) and *David* with his harp appear. Finally in this brief description I will mention the two figures on the bottom tier, those of the martyrs, *St. Alban* and *St. Barnabas*. Except for this very last figure all the designs are by Burne-Jones but *St. Barnabas* and the green foliage (which cleverly all originates from a single root, now hidden by the reredos) are designs of William Morris. His design for the saint is the same one as at St. Wilfrid's in Haywards Heath, where it dates from ten years earlier, both being pre-dated by the use of the design at Linsdale in 1864. You may also wish to know that the *St. Alban* figure is used at St. Wilfrid's church but it is a slightly different design. The figure of *St. Paul* originates from Glasgow where it appeared in 1866.

The notes available inside the church by the Rev. B.S. Hayllar provide a religious interpretation of this spectacular window but opinion has varied over the years about its qualities. Pevsner called it 'outstandingly good' but others have been critical of the small size of the figures making them poorly delineated from a distance. In addition, the foliage background has been questioned, some saying that the use of plain simple quarries would have been preferable. A counter argument could be that its open style compliments the older framework of the window and if one of the purposes of stained glass is to encourage the spiritual development of the congregation, this window surely would achieve this aim. Morris wanted the glass he produced to recall the golden age of medieval times when it was the equivalent of today's cinema. Even now it has the power to be quite magical. Before leaving the building have a look at the astonishingly vivid window showing *The Annunciation* on the south wall of the chancel. This was made in 1903 by Powell to a design by George Parlby about whom little is known unfortunately. **The church is open most days.**

Our next stop is the easily overlooked (4) CHURCH OF ST. PHILIP at Burwash Weald to the south-east. **To get there take the B2101 to join the A267 to Heathfield and then continue along the A265 until you see the village sign, the church being found off the main road on your left.**

Built in 1867 by the industrious architectural partnership of Slater and Carpenter, its creation is due to the efforts of the three Trower sisters who lived nearby on the Hollyhurst estate. Until this building was completed, Church of England worshippers had to travel to Burwash itself, for services. The principal reason for visiting apart from its isolated ambience is to view the three central windows in the apse of the chancel. Outside of these, are two lancets dedicated to the Trower sisters, the one on the north side being a *Resurrection* signed by Jones and Willis. However it is the three Morris like windows that inspire, particularly as they are rather unexpected. None are dated and all employ a foliage background with a border. The central panel showing *Christ and two angels* is perhaps the best, although the other two with their single figures are also impressive. All three windows come from the workshops of James Powell & Sons. Walking back down the church, one is struck by the contrast between its bareness and the warm and vibrant glass at the west end. In this window there are scenes from the life of Christ but it is the use of larger areas of red and blue glass that give a wonderful effect, especially on a sunny day. **The church is open most days.**

A little further along the A265 is (5) BATEMANS, the home of Rudyard Kipling from 1902 until his death in 1936. His previous home in Rottingdean had become too much a subject of public scrutiny and here he found the solitude he sought. The

BATEMANS THE FORMER HOME OF RUDYARD KIPLING - PHOTO BY KIND PERMISSION OF THE NATIONAL TRUST

landscape hereabouts provided the stimulation for some of his most well known books including *Puck of Pook's Hill* and *Rewards and Fairies*.

Kipling's family connections to the Burne-Jones' and to Edward Poynter, another famous Victorian artist have been the subject of many amazed biographers and they do materialise in a number of items in the house. His mother's sister was of course Georgiana Burne-Jones and Kipling often stayed with his aunt and uncle at The Grange, Fulham (their London home) when he was a boy. Kipling's father was also an artist and illustrator who delighted in the work of Morris and Kipling himself was a lifelong friend of the Burne-Jones's.

When touring the house, keep your eyes peeled for important memorabilia and this begins even before you have crossed the threshold. In the porch is the wrought iron bell-pull that had previously been outside The Grange. There is a lovely tale of how Kipling associated this with oases of pleasure (at the Burne-Jones' home) in the otherwise unhappy times of a period in his childhood. On entering the hall at Batemans, you can get a real idea of how the Fulham house looked in its day (it has been demolished) by examining the water-colour to your right by Thomas Rooke, Burne-Jones's assistant. It shows the dining room in 1898 with some Morris & Co. furniture and other paraphernalia. The stained glass panels that are visible to the right of the painting may have been later transferred to North End House at Rottingdean. There is a companion picture to this, which is elsewhere, and shows the drawing room at The Grange with the large oak cabinet now on the other side of the hall in which you now stand. Also in this hall are three water-colours by Edward Poynter, two of which show the exterior of Batemans.

Moving on to a room now known as Elsie Kipling's sitting room, but previously the schoolroom you can see two framed photographs of Kipling's aunts, the Lady's Poynter and Burne-Jones.

Entering the parlour with its charming Tiffany lamps, there is a small picture of Rottingdean actually painted from what was to be Burne-Jones final resting place (by Kipling's cousin Sir Ambrose Poynter). Also in this room is an embroidery of an orange tree that was later made into a curtain. This comes from a design of William Morris dating from about 1860. There are two other similar embroideries in existence - one of a pomegranate tree in the V&A and another showing a lemon tree with the figure of St Catherine at Kelmscott Manor. The one at Batemans may have been completed by Alice Kipling. The three works formed part of a decorative scheme for the drawing room at the Red House that was based on Chaucer's poem Legend of Goode Wimmen which was to have twelve figures with trees around them although the scheme was never completed. Subsequently when Red House was vacated by Morris the panels for the room were returned to their various embroiderers and in addition to the panels already mentioned a three-fold screen originating from the scheme is in the collection of Castle Howard.

After climbing the stairs, do not miss the woodcut of Kipling by William Nicholson which is reputedly to have been made in Burne-Jones' house at Rottingdean in 1897. The study is almost exactly like it was in Kipling's day, and it was here in the last years of his life that he recorded his childhood experiences with Morris and Burne-Jones in his autobiography, Something of Myself. The room contains a portrait of Caroline Kipling by his cousin, Burne-Jones' son, Philip.

Later, there are some nice lithographs by Whistler in the west bedroom and the exhibition room (a conversion from a bedroom) helps to explain the genealogy of the families involved.

Easily missed, but rather delightful, are the three caricatures of the Kiplings' children in the main bedroom. These were drawn by Burne-Jones at Christmas time 1897 and they are shown framed together.

Once outside you can enjoy the same views of the house and surrounding countryside as the visitors in Kipling's time. These included members of the Burne-Jones, Poynter, Baldwin and MacDonald families as well as writers, sculptors and artists of the day.

Trail No. 10 On the Boundary

Points of Interest

(1) DANEHILL - ALL SAINTS CHURCH - A Bodley building with fifteen stained glass windows by Kempe***.

(2) HORSTED KEYNES -CHURCH OF ST. GILES - More Kempe glass **.

(3) WEST HOATHLY - CHURCH OF ST. MARGARET - Stained glass by Kempe and Powells ***.

(4) STANDEN - House designed by Philip Webb with Morris furnishings and art by Burne-Jones, Rossetti and Madox Brown amongst others. (Tel: 01342 323029).

(5) EAST GRINSTEAD - CHURCH OF ST. SWITHIN - Kempe glass and a monument designed by G.E. Street**.

Also: TURNERS HILL - CHURCH OF ST. LEONARD Particularly fine collection of Kempe glass***

POUND HILL - Philip Webb's retirement cottage

STARTING POINT: All Saints church is found (predictably) along the sign-posted Church Lane and is in a prominent position.

HOW TO GET THERE: the village of Danehill is located on the A275 north of Newick close to the gardens at Sheffield Park and the preserved Bluebell Railway

FINISHING POINT: Standen house (National Trust)

REFRESHMENTS: Pubs in the villages, shops and restaurants in East Grinstead, restaurant at Standen

DURATION: This trail runs close to the boundary between East and West Sussex and can be completed as a relaxed half day trip without seeing Standen or the two can be combined, although it is prudent to allow plenty of time for the afternoon visit to the house. Standen is of course the Arts and Crafts showpiece of the county and a full description of the house and gardens, as well as its history is to be found earlier in this book. It is in the care of the National Trust and is open from mid-March to the end of October 11-4.30 (not Monday or Tuesday except in the summer holidays when the house is also open on a Monday). At the very beginning and end of the season it is open at weekends only 11-3 (contact the property for details).

ALL SAINTS CHURCH (1)at Danehill is an important building by G.F. Bodley with his partner Garner and dates from1892. It replaced an earlier church which had only been in existence since 1835 and stood on lower ground, where the war memorial now stands.

In 1875 Herbert Carey Hardy had bought a house nearby called Danehurst in order to live there with his wife Adela Louisa Cassandra Knight. This lady had a family connection to Jane Austen being a granddaughter of the novelist's brother, who had changed his name to Knight. Unfortunately in 1888, Mr. Hardy was killed in an accident and his widow offered to fund the building of a new church in his memory. The church cost nearly £12,000, a not inconsiderable sum and was constructed of local sandstone from Scaynes Hill near Haywards Heath.

Upon entering the building you may first be taken aback by the low light levels. This is due to the high percentage of stained glass and also as a result of Bodley's ideas that churches should be dark and evocative and so add to their mystique. Originally it was lit solely by candles as Bodley felt these would have greater harmony with the architecture. Depending on the illumination available to you it may take a little time to discern the lofty organ positioned high up on the veranda screen and the painted ceilings with their gilded carved bosses. Before moving on to a closer examination of the windows be sure to see the black and white font made of purbeck marble with its impressive oak cover immediately in front of you as you come in. It is nearly ten feet

A DETAIL FROM A KEMPE W1WINDOW IN DANEHILL CHURCH - PHOTO BY AUTHOR

PART OF THE STATUETTE ATTRIBUTED TO MRS G.F. WATTS AT DANEHILL - PHOTO BY AUTHOR

high and was shown at the Victoria and Albert museum in 1972 for an exhibition entitled Victorian Church Art.

There are no less than fifteen stained glass windows all by Kempe although a number are not original to the construction of the church and were done later in conjunction with his partner W E Tower. Kempe was a pupil of Bodley and in the church records are the individualised costs for each window. The standard of them is variable, but they also succeed as an ensemble. Commencing to the right of the entrance, in the south aisle we see a later window of 1916 with the wheatsheaf and tower motif. It shows *St. Stephen* and commemorates a parishioner who died on St. Stephen's Day. Adjacent to this we have three more saints in a larger window that also depicts the three states of Man - *King, Bishop and Peasant* and was installed at the same time as the building's completion.

Moving along, there is a small lancet of *St. Cecilia* with her musical instrument which is appropriately in line with the organ. Records show that this window was paid for by some parishioners and cost £26.

The main east window depicts the *Crucifixion* and more figures of saints whilst high up, the three wheatsheafs of Kempe can be observed. The quatrefoils show some rather fine angels. To the left and right two further good windows show *Mary Magdalen and Michael and All Angels* respectively. Below is the reredos designed by Sir Ninian Comper in the nineteen thirties which now alas is always in an open position due to damage sustained in a break-in attempt.

Returning to the windows an even better example of Kempe is in the chapel in the north east corner of the building. It is a well designed *Nativity* which does however show some war damage (note the light blue glass). The rest of the glass on the northern side is not in the same league but is well worth a look, particularly the one that unusually has a panel showing the grave of a Hardy member in Florida.

Before leaving take a look at the statuette adjacent to the arch that divides the chancel from the chapel which is refuted to be by Mrs. G F Watts. The wife of George Frederick Watts, the ubiquitous Victorian painter and associate of the Pre-Raphaelites, she lived relatively close by at Compton in Surrey. There her work on the cemetery chapel of 1898 uses the sinuous lines of Art Nouveau whereas this work may be based on a painting of her husbands. It commemorates the third son of our Mr. Hardy who was killed in Flanders in 1915. There are three further Kempe windows behind the

glass at the back of the church and two of these show the four Latin fathers with a central *Annunciation*. As you leave, turn around and look up to see the small figure in the niche above the entrance to the porch. In typical Bodley style this was also designed by him and it was placed here in 1907, some years after the church was completed. *The church is usually open.*

Our second church is only a short distance away in the village of Horsted Keynes. *This is found by taking the first road to the left as you leave All Saints.* ST. GILES CHURCH (2) *is on the north side of the village or to the right of the road from Danehill.* The principal interest is again provided by Kempe windows but only three, of which one in particular shines.

The west window in the south aisle shows (a baby) *Jesus being taken to the Temple* by his parents and it is highly finished with intricate details and a carefully constructed background. This is Kempe at his modest best but as frequently occurs there are other examples of later, more inferior work by his Company in close proximity. On the north wall there is a *St. Stephen* of 1910 and the south window of the nave shows a *Nativity,* both these have the wheatsheaf and tower motif.

Other delights around the church include a monument to a boy who appears to have been buried nine months before he was born and the grave of the ex-Prime Minister Harold Macmillan. The former

THE ST. GALAHAD WINDOW AT WEST HOATHLY DESIGNED BY KEMPE & TOWER - PHOTO BY AUTHOR

THE EAST FRONT AT STANDEN - PHOTO BY KIND PERMISSION OF THE NATIONAL TRUST

refers to a Henry Pigott whose memorial tablet on the south side of the chancel states that he was born on the 30th. December 1715 but was buried on the 7th. March of the same year! The explanation for this is that in those days the year changed at the end of March so sadly the infant died when he was just over two months old. **The church is open most days.**

The next stop is West Hoathly high up on a wealden ridge overlooking the Medway valley. **This is reached via Horsted Lane, a minor road heading north from the village. A longer route is possible to take in** ALL SAINTS CHURCH **at Highbrook (reached via Hammingden Lane) where the 1884 building has glass by Clayton and Bell.** This is useful to see in order to differentiate between designers working in the period but whilst Highbrook has merit, it is only occasionally Pre-Raphaelite inspired in any sense.

The (3) CHURCH OF ST. MARGARET, at West Hoathly is mainly thirteenth century and there is an excellent guide available for its varied stained glass. There are good examples of the workshop of Clayton & Bell and there is a dramatic window by the expressionist, Douglas Strachan whose work is in greater quantity at Winchelsea but outside the real focus of this book.

However the lancet window in the south aisle easily fulfils the criteria being a figure of *Sir Galahad* by Kempe and Tower and has their signature motif at the bottom right. It commemorates William Archie Arbuthnot, a 'knight' whose sacrifice was in more recent times-during the slaughter of the First World War.

The tales of King Arthur and the Knights of the Round Table were a great source of inspiration to Victorian artists and in particular to the Pre-Raphaelites. They were the subject of poems by Tennyson and Malory's *Morte d'Arthur* was essential reading for Rossetti, Burne-Jones and others providing the subject matter for many of their

WEBB'S RETIREMENT COTTAGE AT WORTH - PHOTO BY AUTHOR

paintings. Arguably, the sexual narrative was the main theme of interest to them (Arthur's betrayal by Guinevere) although Arthur was seen as a national hero, hence this window's dedication.

Equally as good or even better is the window to the right. The design is by Powells and shows *Christ baptised in the company of John the Baptist*. This fine naturalistic work dates from 1906 and is clearly influenced by the Pre-Raphaelites,

When you leave there is an unusual, vividly blue quatrefoil close to the porch door and adjacent to it, another Kempe window of 1902. This one depicts a woman with a mob cap and is a memorial to Helen Frances who died at sea at the turn of the century. *The church is open most days.*

STANDEN (4) is now within easy reach and described earlier in this book.

The town of East Grinstead provides the conclusion of this trail. It is a place of much history and interest despite its present problems due to heavy traffic and some unsympathetic post war development.

The (5) CHURCH OF ST. SWITHUN contains a good Kempe window of 1899 with a large table shown in its lower panels extending over the three lights. There is also work by Blomfield and Comper although you may find it difficult to see these well in the somewhat gloomy interior. The guidebook also has an illustration of the processional cross that originates from a Burne-Jones design. To conclude, there is a memorial to J. M. Neale, the hymn writer, in the south-east corner of the graveyard, that was designed by the architect G.E. Street in 1866. *The church is open most days.*

ALSO: nearby is another church with impressive Kempe glass for those whose appetite for the same has not yet been satisfied. This is the CHURCH OF ST. LEONARD at Turners Hill, *a short drive away to the west along the B2026.*

The building dates from 1895-7 and inside there are Kempe windows on the north and south side of the chancel as well as glass from 1915 on the south side of the chapel. These all have merit but the best glass is reserved for the main east window. This dates from the construction of the church and shows *Christ in Majesty* with the *Crucifixion* below. The angels in flight that are depicted against a blue patterned sky are very effective

A further short drive gives an opportunity to see where Philip Webb retired to, a few years after creating Standen. ***Follow Turners Hill Road towards Crawley to just west of its bridge over the M23.***

Here you will see a cottage on the right named Caxtons which has a West Sussex heritage plaque on the outside. It was in this traditional building (later extended) that Webb lived from 1900 until his death in 1915. No doubt it was more rural in his time, whereas now in addition to the motorway, it is surrounded by modern housing that uses some of the styling for which he became famous, albeit in rather an eclectic manner.

Trail No. 11 The Downs and the Adur Valley

Points of Interest

(1) HURSTPIERPOINT-CHURCH OF THE HOLY TRINITY - an impressive Victorian building with Hardman & Co. windows.***

(2) WESTMESTON - CHURCH OF ST. MARTIN - a small rural church with much atmosphere and a small Kempe window **.

(3) CLAYTON - church with medieval murals discovered by Kempe. **.

(4) FULKING - MONUMENTS TO JOHN RUSKIN.

(5) HENFIELD - CHURCH OF ST. PETER - more Kempe work **.

(6) TWINEHAM - a charming small church with another Kempe lancet**.

STARTING POINT: the pretty village of Hurstpierpoint about eight miles north of Brighton

HOW TO GET THERE: sign-posted off the A23 just north of Pyecombe.

FINISHING POINT: Hurstpierpoint (circular)

REFRESHMENTS: pubs in most villages with shops in Henfield and Hurstpierpoint.

DURATION: Morning/ afternoon or full day if the further options highlighted are explored.

Also: STREAT CHURCH, SHERMANBURY CHURCH, PARTRIDGE GREEN CHURCH, WEST GRINSTEAD CHURCH (All contain good Kempe stained glass).

Hurstpierpoint is mentioned in the Domesday Book although it has developed particularly since the early nineteenth century. The trail begins at the (1) CHURCH OF THE HOLY TRINITY located centrally and built by Charles Barry between 1843 and 1845. This renowned architect also designed the Houses of Parliament and the nearby Church of St. Peter in Brighton. It replaced the old church of St. Lawrence and some of the correspondence that led to this decision is reproduced in the excellent church guide book.

If you head over to the south aisle after entering the church you will see one of the remnants from the old building- the font which was given its fine decorated cover by Sir Gilbert Scott in 1863. Continue down to the transept to view the John Hardman & Co. windows passing their smaller windows depicting scenes from the life of Christ.

The artist for all the original windows installed in 1860 was John Hardman Powell and there are good examples at both ends of the transept and at the west end, although his window at the opposite end was replaced in 1902 by the present one by Kempe & Co. This no doubt destroyed the previous unity of the windows and the east window (which is dedicated to a casualty of the Boer War), is easily surpassed by another Kempe window of 1917 in the Chapel of St.

THE DECORATED FONT COVER IN THE CHURCH OF THE HOLY TRINITY AT HURSTPIERPOINT - PHOTO BY AUTHOR

Lawrence in the north east corner, This shows the Downs in the background, a sight we will get a closer view of later in the trail. There is further Hardman & Co. glass in the chapel and in the north aisle.

The degree of stained glass does make the interior rather dull on a rainy day but this was an important consideration in Victorian times as Hardman says when he thought there might be insufficient funds; *'the parts not filled (with stained glass) should be darkened to prevent too strong a glare of light'*.

Before leaving there are two further windows of interest, one in the vestry and another more accessible window on the ground floor of the tower by the exit. Both these were once thought to contain medallions of glass by one of the Pre-Raphaelites important influences, the Dutch painter Albrecht Durer. They are set in Victorian glass and are certainly sixteenth century.

The church as a whole offers a glimpse of a typical building of the mid-nineteenth period with good work by Kempe and other artists not very distant from the Pre - Raphaelite circle. *The church is open most days.*

You will now need to find your way to the small (2) CHURCH OF ST. MARTIN *at Westmeston a few miles to the east along the B2116 passing through the village of Ditchling.* It was here that the stone-carver and letter cutter Eric Gill together with his assistant Joseph Cribb settled in 1907. Gill was much influenced by William Morris and was soon joined in Ditchling by the calligrapher Edward Johnston and the printer Hilary Pepler. The village was also the home of a number of important artists during the first half of the twentieth century including Frank Brangwyn who had previously worked with Morris. *The church at Westmeston is by a sharp bend so care needs to be taken when parking.* Inside there are two Clayton & Bell windows in the chancel and a gaudy work by Capronnier in the main window. However the west window of 1890 is by the ubiquitous Kempe & Co. Here he shows the dedicated saint, *St. Martin of Amiens,* cutting his coat in half with his sword to give to a beggar. The church clearly received much attention in Victorian times and it has been called 'over restored' but opinions differ as they do in regard to the quality of the glass. The interior can be dark and there have been calls to replace the present glass with the clear variety. In 1862 medieval wall paintings were discovered but not preserved, although they were faithfully recorded by the then incumbent in the local archaeological collection. **The church is usually open.**

The nearby STREAT CHURCH contains further glass in the Kempe manner including two windows in the south aisle designed by Herbert Bryans.

The next church on the trail provides the opportunity to view some paintings from the same medieval workshop as those lost at Westmeston. **To see these genuine 'pre-Raphaelite' works you will need to go westwards down the minor road marked Underhill Lane which leaves the B2116 at the aforementioned bend in the road to travel along the foot of the South Downs.** THE CHURCH OF ST. JOHN THE BAPTIST(3) is charmingly positioned beneath the windmills named Jack and Jill high up on the summit of the Downs. As you enter the graveyard through the attractive lychgate notice the beautiful gravestone on your left with angelic figures on either side. The building is largely over 900 years old and its interior is dominated by the wall paintings discovered as recently as 1895 by the hardworking Kempe & Co. Their subject is the *Last Judgement* and they reward a close examination. Undoubtedly, they are a good example of the skills of the medieval craftsmen that so impressed Rossetti and in turn Morris and Burne-Jones at the start of their careers. There is little else of

THE ROADSIDE MONUMENT TO JOHN RUSKIN AT FULKING -
PHOTO BY AUTHOR

note, except some geometric designed glass in the chancel and a rather average Kempe window of 1915 depicting the *Crucifixion*. **The church is open most days.**

The next call is in the village of Fulking which can be reached by more than one route. One of the more interesting is to take the narrow road on the other side of the A273 past the historic house of Danny where Prime Minister Lloyd George stayed in 1918, to join the road back through Hurstpierpoint towards the A23. Continue over this busy road until you reach the A281 and head briefly towards Henfield before turning left down to Fulking.

Just beyond the Old Post Office on the right-hand side of the road is a (5) MONUMENT TO JOHN RUSKIN, the art

DETAIL FROM A KEMPE WINDOW AT SHERMANBURY - PHOTO BY AUTHOR

critic and staunch supporter of the Pre-Raphaelites. The residents of the village erected this in grateful thanks for some advice that Ruskin gave them about obtaining a better water supply. Ruskin's interest in geology must have paid dividends because there is also a little pump-house (further on and outside the popular pub, the Shepherd and Dog) which bears a further inscription to this occasion. Both these gothic styled monuments are easily overlooked but indicate the popularity of Ruskin in the late nineteenth century.

Perhaps after some refreshment, continue onwards to Henfield which can be reached by staying on the same road and then going right on the A2037. The (6) CHURCH OF ST. PETER *is found to the west of the High Street.* The interior has a lot of rather average Kempe and Kempe & Co. stained glass. Of more interest is the window in the west corner of the north aisle showing *Fortitude* and *Charity*, the designer being Powell. This dates from 1907 and Alice Barbara, whom the window commemorates is depicted as *St. Barbara* in the quatrefoil above. In the south aisle the window showing *Suffer Little Children* was designed by Mary Lowndes and produced by Powell in 1891. Mary Lowndes worked for some time with Henry Holiday and went on to produce glass with partner Alfred John Dury in the Arts & Crafts tradition. There is also a framed mosaic in the baptistery area that has a Pre-Raphaelite appeal showing *Christ and the children* and dating from 1910. *The church is open regularly. Those wishing to complete the shorter trail should now head towards Twineham and pick up the trail there.*

At this point it is now possible to have a detour to the churches at Shermanbury, Partridge Green and West Grinstead in order to see further good examples of Kempe glass as well as a visit to Shipley which Morris himself visited late in his life, in the company of Wilfrid Scawen Blunt, the poet and erstwhile lover of Jane Morris.

Further north along the A281 but located in grounds to the west of the road (but sign-posted) is SHERMANBURY CHURCH. This has a charming interior with box pews decorated with the names of local farms. There are also many features of a Victorian restoration which are now fortunately, very toned down with age. There are three very nice Art Nouveau influenced mosaic panels on the north side of the chancel with a Kempe window nearby that dates from 1890 and has his three wheatsheafs on a flag above a castle, in the naturalistic background. Two more Kempe windows on either side of the altar commemorate Forrester Britten's parents who it appears died within two months of one another. These suit their location well with their subject extending to the very top of the glass without the need for a border. Although modest, the church typifies the harmony possible in the Pre-Raphaelite interior. *The church is often locked but access/keys are available through the church wardens.*

A little further along the A281, the B2116 goes off to the left and this should be followed to Partridge Green where the CHURCH OF ST. MICHAEL AND ALL ANGELS *is to be found to the west of the A2135 that leaves the village sign-posted West Grinstead.* Although only built in 1890 to cater for the increased population as a result of the arrival of the railways, the flint exterior of the building makes it look older. Inside its bare brick interior the highlight unquestionably is the main east window. A particularly impressive Kempe window of the 1890's with three wide lancets, has bold armoured figures (with quarries behind) that have quirky wings of different colours. This provides quite a contrast to the Kempe windows seen elsewhere with their many smaller saint figures and numerous heraldic shields. *The church is often locked but access is available through the church wardens.*

There is further Kempe glass at WEST GRINSTEAD CHURCH, *a little further along the same road and* SHIPLEY *can be reached by again following the road in the same direction and crossing the busy A24.*

The final stop on this trail is at Twineham, found by returning towards Henfield and taking the B2116 sign-posted to Albourne and then following the signs to the village.

The (6) CHURCH OF ST. PETER *is found at the end of the lane just past the school and almost adjacent to the river.* This rare brick built sixteenth century building will probably provide you with a calm and relaxing conclusion to this trail. Another reason for its inclusion in this book is the modest east window by Kempe. Its subject is another *Annunciation* and it is an early example of his work. Note the roses on the forehead of the *Virgin* which refer to the ancient legend of the Christmas Rose. Also worth a look is the intricately carved Elizabethan family pew and Jacobean pulpit. *The church is open most days.*

The A23 is just a little to the east of Twineham and after readjusting yourself back to the twentieth century leave Kempe behind and make your way back to Hurstpierpoint or from wherever thou did'st come.

Trail No. 12 Worthing Circular

Points of Interest

WORTHING

(1) ART GALLERY - see Holman Hunt's portrait of 'Bianca' and other Pre-Raphaelite works

(2) CHURCH OF ST. PAUL - Morris stained glass in a Greek Revivalist style church***

(3) CHURCH OF ST. ANDREW - a Victorian building full of Kempe glass****

CLAPHAM

(4) CHURCH OF THE BLESSED VIRGIN MARY - a rare Morris tiled reredos****

FINDON

(5) CHURCH OF ST. JOHN THE BAPTIST - Morris tiles****

LANCING

(6) LANCING COLLEGE - awe inspiring chapel with a late Merton Abbey tapestry***

SOUTH LANCING

(7) CHURCH OF ST. MICHAEL AND ALL ANGELS - one late Morris window**

STARTING POINT: Worthing Museum and Art Gallery in Chapel Road.

HOW TO GET THERE: Arriving in Worthing on the main A24 this soon turns into Chapel Road with the gallery on the right.

FINISHING POINT: either South Lancing or return to Worthing

REFRESHMENTS: many in the town centre before moving on to the rural section of the tour.

DURATION: Full day.

Like many a provincial art gallery, WORTHING ART GALLERY AND MUSEUM (1) has little space to display its permanent collection. However, among its works are a number of Pre-Raphaelite pictures as well as paintings by artists associated with the movement at some point in their lives. The star attraction has to be Holman Hunt's *Bianca* completed in 1869. He completed the work whilst staying in Florence in order to finish a monument to his late wife, Fanny. The model was one of the daughters of a family from America who were staying in the city. This was apparently a Miss Lydiard (or in other accounts Margaret Noyes-Bradhurst), whom it seems Hunt considered as a possible partner following the death of his first wife. News of the painting made Edith, Fanny's sister, profoundly jealous although of course it was she that he would eventually marry. Bianca is a character from Shakespeare's *The Taming of the Shrew* although this may be just a pretext for a portrait of an attractive woman in sumptuous clothing. In Hunt's memoirs he describes his working process in regard to the work:

'I commenced this picture in tempera, tracing
out the design and light and shade, as many of
the old masters did, in the end adding the finishing
painting in oil varnish'

A close look at this striking painting reveals the delicacy of Hunt's hand, which is particularly evident in the detailing of the woman's dress and on the mandolin she holds. The gallery has one other work by Hunt, a smaller pastel completed about six years earlier, entitled *Dr. Edward Wilson as a Boy*. The subject is Hunt's nephew and godson who was born in 1857.

In the collection, there is also a drawing by Frederick Sandys entitled *Sweet Thoughts* (1894) which is one of his typically skilled studies of women but with no obvious mythological reference on this occasion. There is also a drawing by Simeon Solomon of *Perseus* from 1892 as well as a landscape by Albert Goodwin depicting *Rye Port*. Walter Crane is represented in the collection by his water-colour of another Sussex scene, *Winchelsea Church*. The gallery also has in its possession works by Brabazon (Eastern scenes), a couple of late Brangwyn's, and works by William Henry Hunt, Edward Lear, A.Morgan Price and Edward Stott.

The local artist Averil Burleigh (1884-1949)who lived in Brighton for much of her life is represented by one lovely work, *Madonna of the Peach Trees*. She painted a number of works with literary themes and in the thirties often used tempera as in the Worthing picture. The work owes much to the paintings of the Nazarenes, the artist group that so influenced the Pre-Raphaelites early on in their development.

Not all these works will be on display at any one time, although there is a room devoted to the permanent collection, so it is well worth phoning ahead to check and you may be able to make arrangements to view paintings not currently shown. **The gallery and museum are open Tue-Sat 10-5.**

The second stop on the trail is provided by (2) ST. PAUL'S CHURCH **a little to the south of the gallery, across the road.** This distinctive building of the Regency era is (at the time of writing) closed due to a leaking roof but there are plans to reopen it in the near future. This neo-classical church has a Royal Coat of Arms as Princess Amelia attended service here whilst staying in the town. Inside, at the east end are two unexpectedly large panels of Morris glass that date from 1933. On the left, in red is *The Good Shepherd* from a design by Henry Dearle. Opposite is the figure of *St. Paul* in blue, from an original design by Burne-Jones. The rather pleasing designs include acanthus plants that form a frame for the two figures. It is interesting to compare the depiction of *The Good Shepherd* with another Morris window of the same subject in

'MADONNA OF THE PEACH TREES' BY AVERIL BURLEIGH - PERMISSION OF WORTHING MUSEUM AND ART GALLERY

the nearby CHURCH OF THE HOLY TRINITY. This window (on the north side and first from the west end) is from a design by Burne-Jones and was installed in the same year. **Both these churches may unfortunately be locked but it is possible to obtain access through the Parish Office.**

ST. ANDREW'S CHURCH (3) *in Victoria Road is our next visit where a cornucopia of superb Kempe glass is to be found.* The building was completed in 1888 by Arthur Blomfield, the distinguished architect. All but a couple of windows in the south aisle are by Kempe and even these were completed following his death by Kempe & Co. Ltd. When you enter the church there is a sense of great richness amid the spaciousness, achieved not only by the glass but also by the stone carvings of Harry Hems, and the painted ceilings and screens. Of particular merit is the north window in the Lady Chapel showing the *Nativity*, as well as the narrow lancets in the apse. In the ex- choir school attached to the church, there is further Kempe glass that was rescued from the now demolished All Souls church in Brighton. Although much of the glass is

A DETAIL OF THE FIGURE OF THE GOOD SHEPHERD IN ST PAULS CHURCH IN WORTHING - PHOTO BY AUTHOR

comparatively late work it is striking how it creates a unified and harmonious whole. **The church is occasionally locked and access is possible through the church wardens.**

It is time to leave the town of Worthing and head out into the country. The village of Clapham is found to the north-west off the A280 which in turn is signposted from the A27 road to Arundel. The (4) CHURCH OF THE BLESSED VIRGIN MARY *lies in an isolated position to the north of the village.*

This 12th. Century church was restored by Sir George Gilbert Scott in 1873-4, some seven years after his work on nearby Findon, where we shall shortly visit. These two churches share a unique legacy, they are the only ecclesiastical buildings to contain a Morris reredos of painted tiles. The one at Clapham shows (from left to right) the four archangels, *Gabriel, Michael, Raphael* and *Uriel.* This centre panel is the largest produced as a single unit and was made at a time of great technical expertise within the Company. The colouring of the tiles has therefore remained vivid. The figures stand before a mixture of fruit trees, willow, roses and vines. The archangels only appear together elsewhere at Wigan, where there is a main window showing them. However single figures and tracery figures occur nearer to home, for example, the figure of *Raphael* can be seen in glass at Haywards Heath. The archangels are flanked by tiles with what is now known as the *'Clapham Vine'* design which although inferior in quality, still complement the main panel appropriately. There is a local story about these wonderful tiles which deserves repeating. Apparently an influential woman in the village disliked the tiles and so covered them with a blue curtain, resulting in them becoming 'lost' until rediscovered more recently. Written records about the tiles were thought to refer to Clapham in London before experts found them. It seems that the actions of this lady may also have helped the tiles to remain in good condition, and means that their whereabouts are still relatively unknown. The stained glass in the church fails to impress but the marble and gold pulpit and screen are worth a look even if they are not to everyone's taste. **The church is open regularly.**

The short trip to Findon with its own Morris reredos highlights how it must have been local enthusiasm for the Company's tiles that led to two commissions from such a close geographical area. The (5) CHURCH OF JOHN THE BAPTIST *lies close to the manor house at the end of a private road going off the A24 Worthing to London road.* The building was the subject of a Scott restoration in 1867.

The reredos is perhaps slightly less impressive than Clapham, consisting of two sets of three angels either side of a curtain on the east chancel wall. Morris designed twelve such figures that were used frequently in stained glass work. The figures used here carry (from left to right) a long flared pipe, a dulcimer, a harp, another long flared pipe, a V shaped organ and another harp. The flowers shown are what has come to be called, the *'Findon Buttercup'* and *'Findon Daisy'*.

The tiles are not in as good condition as those at Clapham which is at least partly explained by them having an unstable glaze to begin with. Their appearance is also not helped by the fact that a central wooden reredos with panels by Kempe has been removed at some stage. This is now at St. Mary's House in Bramber (open to the public) after spending time in a local barn.

PART OF THE MORRIS TILED REREDOS IN CLAPHAM CHURCH - PHOTO BY AUTHOR

None of the church's glass is really Pre-Raphaelite but that in the north-west corner is good and there is a pleasing Victorian pulpit, although the modern flooring and furniture aren't very complementary. *The church is often locked but access is available through the church wardens.*

The penultimate stop on this tour is at (6) LANCING COLLEGE CHAPEL *which is spectacularly positioned above the Adur valley and visible from the A27 road near Shoreham. Take the A24 south from Findon and then the A27 towards Brighton.*

The exterior of this fine gothic building is quite awesome even though it is still unfinished in regard to the original intentions of its architect, R.H. Carpenter. Work began on the building in 1868 and the stone used came from a local quarry at Scaynes Hill. Inside one should not miss the stalls at the side of the nave that were designed by Walter Tower with their canopies by Sir George Gilbert Scott. The huge tapestries behind the high altar came from Merton Abbey but date from a time long after William Morris founded his works there. They were designed by a Lady Chilston in 1933 and took four years to complete. Perhaps something of the simplicity of early Pre-Raphaelite paintings is evident but a lot of imagination is required. In the crypt downstairs are what appears to be Clayton & Bell windows (in the central apse)in memory of the architect. In addition, there is a rather nice alabaster reredos in the Founder's Chapel that was designed by Carpenter's business partner, Bernard Ingelow as well as good glass by Clayton & Bell. *The chapel is open From 10-4 on most days.*

The final destination is the (7) CHURCH OF ST. MICHAEL AND ALL ANGELS *at South Lancing (sign-posted from the A27).* This very modest building has a Morris east window in the south chapel. A late work dating from 1927 it shows (in the left light), *St. Clement* and adjacent, *St. Valentine*. Both designs are by Henry Dearle but redrawn from original designs by Burne-Jones. They are rather appealing especially in the relatively bare surroundings of the interior. *The church may be locked but access is possible through the church wardens. This concludes the tour with Worthing a short drive away along the coastal A259.*

Trail No. 13 Petworth and thereabouts

Points of Interest

(1)   FITTLEWORTH - ST. MARY'S CHURCH - Kempe glass**

(2)   SELHAM CHURCH - Plaque adapted from a Watts painting**

(3)   TILLINGTON - ALL HALLOWS CHURCH - Burne-Jones windows and more stained glass inspired by Holman Hunt's 'Light of the World'.***

(4)   PETWORTH HOUSE - original wallpapers and furnishings by Morris. (Tel: 01798 342207).

Also: CHURCH OF ST. AGATHA AT COATES**

STARTING POINT: The church at Fittleworth, north of the village.

HOW TO GET THERE: sign-posted from the A283 between Pulborough and Petworth. It is essential to have a car.

FINISHING POINT: Petworth House (National Trust)

REFRESHMENTS: pubs in all the villages and a café/restaurant at Petworth House.

DURATION: morning/afternoon or leisurely full day -

ST. MARY'S CHURCH (1)at Fittleworth underwent restoration during the 1870's and although the church guide calls this work 'inferior gothic style', the work may have been necessary due to the building being in a poor state. It seems that the ubiquitous Kempe was here, as the same guide refers to an old oak chest by the south door that used to belong to him, although this could not be located at the time of writing. Kempe's windows are however easier to find, marked as they are with his wheatsheaf signature. That in the north-east corner has a nice simplicity, a single light with a figure of *St. Cecilia*. There is a further Kempe & Co. window as well as a Kempe window in the south aisle. They vary a little in quality, which is to be expected but Kempe is only rarely poor in execution. Perhaps the best feature of the church is its peacefulness, whilst inside it is almost possible to visualise Kempe at work although it is not definite that he visited the building. ***The church is open most days.***

A short trip to the west along the A272 (turn left at Halfway Bridge) and (2) SELHAM CHURCH *is reached.* Easy to pass, a visit inside will help one to appreciate the enormous influence of the Pre-Raphaelites and their circle, right into the twentieth century. On the north wall is a small tablet in honour of a victim of The Great War and dated 1918. This is an adaptation of a G.F.Watts painting illustrating *Sir Galahad with a Horse.* Watts had many contacts throughout his life with his younger contemporary, Rossetti and as can be seen, shared on occasion similar subject matter. The painting was also used as the basis for a later Morris window at Freshwater on the Isle of Wight to a design by Henry Dearle. **The church is open most days.**

Rejoin the A272 and head back towards Petworth to arrive at Tillington. ALL HALLOWS CHURCH (3) with its unusual Scots Crown spire appears in a painting by Turner, completed when he was resident at Petworth House. The north aisle was completed in the first half of the nineteenth century when the rest of the church was renovated, for Lord Egremont, Turner's patron and occupant of the House. However, it is the south aisle that contains a window in memory of a member of the Mitford family that owned many of the houses in the village. We have two lights showing *Christ as the Good Shepherd* and a *Light of the World* in a combination seen before. The latter is one of the representations more faithful to the original Holman Hunt picture and is delightful in muted sunlight. The designer was Heaton Butler & Bayne and although a Pre-

TILING BASED ON A WATTS PAINTING IN
SELHAM CHURCH - PHOTO BY AUTHOR

Raphaelite subject the *Light of the World* was not produced by Morris & Co. until well after Morris's death. However high up on the west wall there is a Morris & Co roundel window showing the Second Coming. This *Dies Domini* with Christ seated in white robes showing his wounds, is a design by Burne-Jones and dates from 1906. Its unusual position, isolated as it is, gives it a certain celestial air. **The church is open most days.**

PETWORTH HOUSE (4) **lies within walking distance of the church or the National Trust car park is a short drive away through the town of Petworth.** This magnificent property was the southern home of the powerful Percy family from about 1150. In the seventeenth century, the sixth Duke of Somerset married into the family and he is mainly responsible for much of how the house appears today. The next century saw the house pass by marriage to the Earls of Egremont who built up its art collection with the third Earl adding a sculpture gallery to the house. In the nineteenth century, the house passed to the Wyndham family and it is these occupants that provide a Morrisian connection. Percy and Madeline Wyndham were both involved in the Arts and Crafts Movement and used to spend time at Petworth with their children, where Henry, Percy's elder brother was resident. They commissioned Philip Webb to build them a house in Wiltshire called Clouds, which had it survived intact would now be seen as a showpiece of the Movement to rival Standen. Percy and Madeline were no doubt the reason for Morris & Co. being commissioned to provide furnishings for some of the rooms in Petworth House. Mrs. Wyndham's dressing room has original wallpaper and also curtains and upholstery by the Company. The bedroom corridor also has what may well be a reprint of a Morris wallpaper. In the Trellis Suite is a portrait by G.F. Watts of Percy's brother, Henry Wyndham, 2nd. Lord Leconfield.

Although the Morris work is a comparatively minor addition to the house it is an interesting one, and rather unexpected. Whilst looking at the rest of this incredible home, it is possible to see a number of paintings attributed to, or by artists who were inspirational to the Pre-Raphaelites. These include the medieval artists, Memling and Van Der Weyden as well as important works by William Blake. There are also some pictures by Madeline Percy who was herself a talented artist. *The house is open from April to September from 1-5 except on Thursday and Fridays. The rooms with the Morris decoration are only open on Tuesday and Wednesday.*

A pleasant but not essential addition to this tour is the tiny CHURCH OF ST. AGATHA at Coates. This hamlet lies to the south-east of Petworth.

Inside the simple white interior are two lancet windows depicting two of the Apostles which are by Kempe and date from 1898. There is still an exhilarating sense of remoteness that prevails in this building,that has changed so little as the centuries have passed. *The church is open most days.*

BURNE - JONES ROUNDEL AT TILLINGTON - PHOTO BY AUTHOR

Trail No. 14 The Arun Valley

Points of Interest:

(1) BINSTED - CHURCH OF ST. MARY - Henry Holiday stained glass that is mysteriously recorded in the records of Morris & Co. despite being produced by Powells. **

(2) SLINDON - CHURCH OF ST. MARY - Glass and reredos inspired by Morris***

(3) MADEHURST - CHURCH OF ST. MARY MAGDALEN -Remains of a Burne-Jones window that was largely destroyed in the last war. ***

(4) AMBERLEY - CHURCH OF ST. MICHAEL - Glass by Anning Bell and other work by followers of Christopher Whall and by Eric Gill. ***

(5) BURPHAM - CHURCH OF ST. MARY - A version of 'The Light of the World' in glass and some good Powell windows. ****

Also: BURY - Home of John Galsworthy

CLYMPING - The church that the Burne-Jones and Morris families visited.

STARTING POINT: Arundel Cathedral is clearly visible on high ground on the west side of the town (easy access via the roundabout of the A27 & A284)

HOW TO GET THERE: The town is located on the A27 between Chichester and Worthing

FINISHING POINT: Arundel.

REFRESHMENTS: plenty of restaurants and tea-shops in Arundel. Pubs at Burpham and Amberley.

DURATION: Morning/afternoon or leisurely full day.

This trail starts at Arundel, a popular location on account of its imposing castle and riverside position. There is a magnificent view of the town when approaching from the east and although its magical appearance is mainly a nineteenth century creation, the town retains a certain earlier charm. One of the most prominent buildings is the CATHEDRAL OF OUR LADY AND ST. PHILIP HOWARD which is found high up on the west side of town. Although it contains nothing with a direct Pre-Raphaelite connection, it is interesting as a nineteenth century copy of fourteenth century French Gothic style. The architect was Joseph Hansom, more famous perhaps as the inventor of the Hansom cab, so ubiquitous in the Sherlock Holmes novels. Although the cathedral has been criticised for being an uninspired recreation, it does impress with its sheer size and gives some idea of the effect that the genuine artefact had on Messrs. Ruskin, Morris and Burne-Jones on their Normandy travels. The design of much of the stained glass by John Hardman is striking, (perhaps not surprisingly as he worked with Pugin) and the recent cleaning of the stonework only adds to the cathedral's grandeur. *The cathedral is open most days.*

Leaving Arundel our first stop is the little (1) BINSTED CHURCH, *the first of many on this trail dedicated to St. Mary. It is found by following the main A27 in the direction of Chichester and taking the sign-posted minor road on your left after a couple of miles.* The church has a rather nice rural location and inside at the east end are three Powell windows that date from 1869. The figures were designed by Henry Holiday who succeeded Burne-Jones at the London based company, James Powell and Sons. He was a man of forthright opinion whose work is invariably of good quality. His painting *'The First meeting of Dante and Beatrice'* is a Pre-Raphaelite masterpiece and was very popular in its time. The grisaille patterning of these windows are by another Powell designer, the architect Sir Thomas (T.G.) Jackson and the same Company supplied the chancel flooring. *The church is open most days.*

Our next port of call is the village of Slindon to the north-west which is reached by crossing both the A27 and A29 on minor roads. The second CHURCH OF ST. MARY (2) of our trail was restored in 1866 and this work is described in typically direct language by Pevsner as 'shocking'. The perpetrator was the same T.G. Jackson who also designed some of the stained glass here. The five lancets of the east window are designed by him and produced by Powell and are in memory of members of the Tilley and Izard families and show the influence of Morris at that time, as do the other chancel windows with their predella like scenes from the life of Christ. These include an *Adam and Eve* and a faded *Noah's Ark* that are undated.

Also of interest is the mosaic reredos depicting the *Four Evangelists* and the *Ten Commandments*. No doubt this together with the coloured floor tiles and pleasantly decorated organ pipes date from the time of the Rev. Chantler Izard's restoration initiative. Before you leave you may wish to view the famed wooden effigy of Sir Anthony St. Leger, the only one in Sussex and dating from the sixteenth century. There is also a memorial by Sir Richard Westmacott. *The church is open most days.*

We now travel to the nearby village of Madehurst via the A29 eastwards and along the first minor road on the left. MADEHURST CHURCH (3) was originally a shepherds chapel built by the monks of Tortington Priory. It has further connections to our previous two churches- it's another St. Mary's (but Magdalen) and our old friend T.G. Jackson performed a major restoration job on it in 1864. Despite this the church is quietly atmospheric, although this has not always been the case. On the 12th. July 1944 a V1 flying bomb landed in a hedge about 300 yards east of the church. It damaged the Vicarage and also blew in the main east window of the church. In addition

THE ATMOSPHERIC INTERIOR OF MADEHURST CHURCH - PHOTO BY AUTHOR

a Burne Jones window was too badly shattered to be repaired although the smaller light above can still be seen (on the south side of the nave, second from the west).

It shows an *Angel with a T-shaped dulcimer* and there is also some pattern work in the two slit lights. A little imagination is needed to visualise how the larger windows would have looked. They showed the *Four Evangelists* in the same design as the famous Burne Jones window in Jesus College, Cambridge and dated from 1876.

Be sure to see the three charming lancets in the chancel with their single figures and inscriptions that were gifted by the children of a Mr. And Mrs. J.O. Fletcher of nearby Dale Park in memory of their parents. They were designed by Henry Holiday at Powell in 1890. There is also some impressive animal carving on the pews as well as stonework to be enjoyed.

The organ is by Henry Willis a well known figure in his field who was also apparently responsible for the organs in Westminster Abbey and St. Pauls. *If the church is locked the key is available from the house at the far end of the lane to the left of the church.*

When you finally decide to leave this idyll continue to drive in an eastward direction until you arrive at the A29 where you should go left. Then at the big roundabout take the B2139 through some stunning scenery down to Amberley. After arriving in the village, the (4) CHURCH OF ST. MICHAEL *is found by taking the first road to the left.* Before entering the building the churchyard surrounding it has a surprising amount of interest.

The artist Edward Stott (1859-1918) lived and worked in this charmingly anachronistic village for over thirty years. Principally a painter of rural life, in later years he painted an increasing number of biblical subjects using the Sussex landscape

THE BRONZE RELIEF BY FRANCIS DERWENT WOOD IN AMBERLEY CHURCHYARD - PHOTO BY AUTHOR

as his setting. A number of his works can be viewed in the house at Standen and although he is not considered to be a follower of the Pre-Raphaelites and the pictures are not original to the house, their presence there is testimony to their appropriateness. There is a memorial to Stott by the Royal Academician, Francis Derwent Wood in the churchyard (1918) as well as an equally impressive bas-relief of bronze also made by Wood (1909) to commemorate himself and his wife.

There is a further memorial to Stott, this time inside the church. This is in the form of a stained glass window opposite the south door, by an acknowledged Pre-Raphaelite sculptor and designer, Robert Anning Bell and dating from 1919. The central section is taken from a Stott painting and shows the *Descent from the Cross*, most of the figures being drawn from local residents. The figure of Christ was however taken from a professional model who is said to have been paid 6d. a session. Bell was a student at the Royal Academy from 1879 and later shared a studio with another sculptor who for a time was inspired by the Pre-Raphaelite ideal, George Frampton. Bell is best known for his small plaster reliefs of mainly female figures but after 1907 increasingly concentrated on other decorative art such as mosaic and stained glass (as here).

The other Victorian glass in the church includes a *Dorcas* and a *Charity* but are not particularly inspired. It is worth taking a look at the window in the south aisle that shows St. *Edith* which was done by Veronica Whall in the early thirties. Together with the Stratton memorial on the west wall (by Eric Gill) these show work completed by later admirers of Morris and his contemporaries.

The book illustrator Arthur Rackham lived at nearby Houghton House and he is also commemorated by a plaque in the churchyard made by the sculptor John Skelton. Although Rackham has no direct connections to the Pre-Raphaelites, there is a clear line connecting Morris's innovative Kelmscott Press illustrations to Rackham's success in the same genre forty years later. **The church is open most days.**

Our final stop is in the village of Burpham which can be reached more directly on foot by going over the Downs in a southerly direction. For the less brave the only access by car is along a three mile cul-de-sac road off the A27 a little to the east of Arundel.

BURPHAM CHURCH (5) is given a mention in the Domesday Book and is a veritable treasure-trove for the detective historian. In 1869 it was the subject of a sympathetic restoration by yes, T. G. Jackson and is yes, another St. Mary (The Virgin). Amongst its many Victorian windows is a Kempe one of standard fare to the left of the entrance below the tower. In memory of Robert Foster, it has a familiar design showing *Isaiah* with *St. Michael* and *King David*, although the lower section is partially obscured behind the organ. Of greater interest are the three small lancets of the south aisle made by Powell in 1885 and designed by J.W. Brown. To look at these is almost like seeing Holman Hunt's *'The Light of the World'* painting retold in the manner of a triptych. In the first panel (inscribed 'I am the Light of the World') the figure of Christ is holding a lantern very like the one used by Hunt with the second window bearing the familiar quotation 'Behold I Stand at the Door and Knock'. The best panel is the final one with the inscription 'Behold the Man' with its crown of thorns and instruments of the Passion.

However the most inspiring window has to be the Powell window opposite on the north wall. On the right hand side next to a later window of 1891 it depicts the three figures of *Mary Magdalen, the Virgin Mary and Mary of Bethany.* Dated 1881 and in memory of the Drewitts, it is particularly fine. The rose window with a geometric design is also worth a peek as are the many examples of Victorian carving on the pews, pulpit and lectern. *The church is open most days.*

Now make your way back into Arundel down the valley of the river for some deserved refreshment.

ADDITIONAL PLACES OF INTEREST IN THE AREA:

BURY: John Galsworthy spent the last years of his life at Bury House where a blue plaque commemorates this. The novelist and dramatist is now best remembered for 'The Forsyte Saga' a series of novels following the fortunes of a Victorian family from the late nineteenth to early twentieth century.

CLYMPING: Whilst having a holiday at Littlehampton in September 1864 the Burne-Joneses visited the church here. They found it rather neglected with worm-ridden furniture and a very damp floor. They took particular note of a tiny gravestone in the memory of a child and how a sheep-dog expertly led a flock of sheep out of the graveyard. In many ways the church has been surprisingly unaffected by the subsequent twentieth century and the building remains one of the more interesting in the county.

A DETAIL FROM THE ANNING BELL STAINED GLASS AT AMBERLEY - PHOTO BY AUTHOR

Trail No. 15 Chichester and Bognor

Points of Interest:

(1) CHICHESTER CATHEDRAL - Glass by Kempe and a commemorative plaque to the man.****

(2) LAVANT - CHURCH OF ST.MARY - Kempe glass***

(3) BOXGROVE PRIORY - Arts and Crafts glass by Mary Lowndes***

(4) EASTERGATE PARISH HALL - Murals by Byam Shaw

(5) SOUTH BERSTED - Church with outstanding stained glass by Powells ***

(6) BOGNOR REGIS - Where Rossetti spent a wild winter and where his studio can be seen (externally).

(7) FELPHAM - Home to William Blake at the beginning of the nineteenth century

(8) OVING - CHURCH OF ST. ANDREW - More fine glass by Powells***.

STARTING POINT: Chichester Cathedral

HOW TO GET THERE: The city is located on the A27 between Havant and Arundel

FINISHING POINT: Chichester

REFRESHMENTS: pubs at Oving and Felpham and many restaurants and cafes in Chichester and Bognor.

DURATION: Full day.

We start in Chichester, a wonderful city set within its Roman walls and where Keats, that much admired poet, once had lodgings. Amid the grand buildings from differing eras lies the grandest of them all, the (1) CATHEDRAL and it is here the trail begins.

On the 12th. December 1895 less than a year before he died, Morris wrote a letter to the editor of The Times about the then proposed rebuilding of the cathedral's north-west tower. As the secretary of the Society for the Protection of Ancient Buildings (SPAD) he was concerned that such work would destroy older parts of the building as he felt was the case in other examples of Victorian 'restoration'. He wrote *'a wound inflicted in any part of such a building as one of our cathedrals is felt throughout its whole body, and may have a most prejudicial effect in disturbing its equilibrium'.*

However the work was completed in 1901 by the architect J.L. Pearson. This together with the undoubted need for the reconstruction of the central tower in 1861(the original became dangerous) by Sir Gilbert Scott and Slater were the main Victorian changes to the building.

Inside, there is a wealth of architectural and artistic interest including sculptures by Flaxman and Gibson and more contemporary work by Chagall, Piper, Sutherland and Hans Feibusch.

In the choir crossing is the large and not unimpressive gothic revivalism of Slater and Carpenter's bishop's throne. This together with Sir George Gilbert Scott's restored tomb chest in the south aisle conjures up perfectly the feeling behind the romantic medievalism of many Victorian artists.

Moving on to the retrochoir there is some fine Kempe glass high up in the east window. The scenes depicted include a *Crucifixion* and *Adam and Eve* and are particularly rich in their colouring. It is interesting to compare them to the Clayton & Bell glass in the Lady Chapel (you can do this at the same time) where the glass is successful because of its uniformity but has much less liveliness. Less of a triumph is Kempe's glass in the south-east chapel where he depicts *Christ with St. Mary and St. Joseph* rather drably.

Moving to the south transept you will see the three bay stone screen and tomb of Bishop Stratford (1337-62) and it is in this area that we have a further two reminders of Kempe. First, there is a brass (on the floor) completed by him in 1888 which shows the man's command of yet another skill. It is a very pleasing design which is easily overlooked, whilst on the wall adjacent is a tablet commemorating Kempe, by his partner W.E.Tower, following his death in 1907.

Finally look out for a monument to Bishop Dunford further down the south aisle. This is by old friends Bodley and Garner and shows their talent in rendering the intricate details of gothic carving - even if Pevsner does describe it as being 'stone dead'!
The cathedral is open at regular times.
We now leave the city and go north along the A286 to East Lavant which is sign-

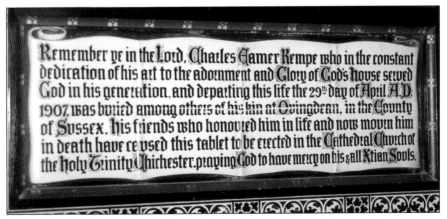

THE COMMEMORATIVE PLAQUE TO KEMPE IN CHICHESTER CATHEDRAL - PHOTO BY AUTHOR

posted to the right. The (2) CHURCH OF ST. MARY *is then found on the left.* It has an attractive brick tower and was restored in 1863. Amongst its Victorian glass there are three of particular merit. The window in the north aisle at the east end is in memory of Mary Norman Paxton and is clearly Morris inspired but rather lacking in its execution. Of greater beauty are the two windows that face each other north and south of the main east window in the chancel. On the left is glass by Powells that shows *St. Gabriel* and *St. Michael* with four putti heads above which are much in the style of those at East Hoathly. Sprinkled throughout are Tudor roses and there is a wonderfully rich foreground that includes the trampled dragon. Opposite is a finely detailed glass of 1883 by Kempe and shows four scenes from the biblical story of Gehazi. It is a beguiling window and benefits from a bright day to give an almost 3-D effect. It is possible that the window in the south transept depicting *David lamenting the deaths of Saul and Jonathan* is by Henry Holiday dating from 1875. The building is otherwise modestly charming and has a fine stone and marble reredos. *The church is occasionally locked but access is possible through the church wardens.*

Our next stop is (3) BOXGROVE PRIORY *which is reached by going down the minor road opposite the entrance to Lavant church. When this reaches the A285 you should travel left and then turn right at Halnaker.* As you enter the building be prepared for what is a stunning interior with its painted ceiling and purbeck marble columns. There is a truly massive east window by the Victorian designer O'Connor that is spectacular mainly due to its sheer size but a little uninspired. It is certainly superior to his window on the right where the lead is not integral to the design and to the rather disappointing Kempe & Co. window depicting *St. George* and dated 1914 with the motif of a wheatsheaf and tower.

The main reason for anyone visiting Boxgrove with an interest in how the Pre-Raphaelites influenced design into the twentieth century lies in the four small single lancets in the south aisle. These little jewels depict *Mary and a Centurion* amongst other characters and were executed by Mary Lowndes in 1907. She was a leading exponent of the Arts and Crafts Movement and it is not difficult to see Morris's influence together with a number of other stylistic inspirations. *The priory is open most days.*

The next port of call is to be found amongst the suburbia that is now Eastergate. Continue on in the same direction and turn left at the roundabout with the A27 before going right towards Aldingbourne. This road leads into Eastergate and you should look for the (4) PARISH HALL *easily missed on the right.* Inside this inconspicuous building with its wooden panelling and small scaled classical columns are eleven little known murals, some of which were painted by the artist Byam Shaw.

He was a latter day Pre-Raphaelite whose most famous work was a painting called 'Boer War 1900' actually completed in 1901. It shows a grieving widow whose husband has been lost in the war, amidst a finely detailed English countryside and is reminiscent of Millais' *'Ophelia'*. It also has a similar theme of death and loss contrasting with the beauty of nature. To underline the point it was exhibited with an inscription from a poem by Christina Rossetti - *'Last Summer green things were greener/ Brambles fewer, the blue sky bluer'*. The picture's popularity led to a mini-revival of the style some fifty years after its initial appearance.

The murals at Eastergate show historical scenes with backgrounds from the local area and some were completed by Shaw in 1909 and others by artists such as Eva Day and Barbara Chamier, sometimes later. The murals show *St. Wilfrid landing at Selsey in 680AD, Queen Elizabeth I in Cowdray Park, Charles II passing through Houghton on*

ONE OF THE MURALS TO BE FOUND IN EASTERGATE PARISH HALL - PHOTO BY AUTHOR

his way to Shoreham and the 'father of cricket' *Dick Newland* by Slindon Pond. The remaining panels show *King Harold hunting wild boar, Arundel castle in 1574, a regiment of Dragoons at Walberton House prior to Waterloo* and the novelist *Charlotte Smith at Eartham House in 1792 whilst being sketched by Romney.* As well as two essentially non-pictorial panels there is one wider panel by Shaw that originally would have run the full width of the hall. This is perhaps the finest mural depicting *Sir Ralph Hopton optimistically trying to relieve the besieged Arundel Castle with two cannons now resident in Fontwell Gardens.*

It could be argued that the style of some of the murals have only a tenuous connection to Pre-Raphaelitism but they are charming and of historical importance to those interested in the subsequent development of the artist. **At the time of writing the keyholders details are shown in the windows of the hall should the building be locked.**

It is possible to now go directly to Oving if a shorter route is required but the trail will now move on to South Bersted, the next stop. Go back along the same road and then continue on down the A29 in the direction of Bognor Regis. The church is found down a road on the right hand side after entering the suburb. Despite its unpromising setting (5) SOUTH BERSTED CHURCH contains one of the county's finest Victorian windows supplied by Powells. The main east window dates from 1880 and commemorates the Rev. Eedle who was vicar at the church for over fifty years. In three huge lights it shows two incidents from Mary Magdalene's life to whom the building is dedicated. On the right is her Conversion whilst the left light shows her shock at seeing the *Risen Christ* (notice the angel above has a crown of thorns). The

THE ROSSETTI STUDIO AT BELMONT PLACE IN BOGNOR REGIS - PHOTO BY AUTHOR

emotion is fairly tangible, exaggerated by the bright colours (including haloes with a red outer ring)but it all works wonderfully. It is underlined by the inscriptions *'Touch Me Not / He Is Risen Indeed/ I Will Give You Rest'.*

The three windows on the south side of the chancel are so poor in comparison and were (unbelievably) also supplied by Powells, according to the church guide. In the east end of the south aisle is a small window inscribed St. John and dated 1905 which is attractive in a more modest way. ***The church can be locked and access is possible through the church wardens.***

Just down the road is the seaside resort of Bognor which was home to Rossetti during one of his darker spells in 1875(see the earlier section in this book). On a wild day it is possible to imagine him walking along the beach in the direction of Selsey his body bent into the wind. I found no trace of Aldwick House but it is easy to spot the studio he moved to in town when the wind grew too much. This is located at (6)BELMONT LODGE (now altered) in the street of the same name. There is a helpful blue heritage plaque outside.

A little to the east along the A259 is the former village of (7) FELPHAM ***now attached to the housing developments of Bognor.*** It was here that one of the heroes of the Brotherhood lived for a short while at the beginning of the nineteenth century as a guest of a popular writer of the time called William Hayley. This was William Blake, the visionary poet and engraver. In 1800 he was persuaded by Hayley to move into a vacant cottage in the village with a promise from his friend, that he would find him work and further commissions for engraving.

Blake stayed three years and the time he spent in Felpham was not without incident. On one occasion he got into a violent argument with a soldier who later accused him of shouting anti-royalist views and a court case followed. It was a time of great national anxiety with Napoleon poised to invade the country. Blake was acquitted of the charge of sedition but it must have been a worrying time for him.

The cottage that Hayley extended to become Turret House is no longer there but a blue heritage plaque shows its location. Similar plaques are in evidence outside the Fox Inn (down Limmer Lane), the place where the disagreement with the military occurred, and at Blake's cottage. This is found by continuing past the pub into Blake's Road where his cottage is on the left. A look at Felpham church will reveal a monument to Hayley on the north wall of the chancel. Interestingly, before moving to this seaside village Hayley lived at Eartham House where he entertained such celebrities of the time as Flaxman the sculptor, Cowper the poet and Gibbons the author. You may remember that one of the murals in the hall at Eastergate shows the Sussex poet Charlotte Smith at the house where she was another occasional visitor.

Now drive back towards Chichester but before we complete this trail it is worth taking a short detour off the A259. Follow the signs to the village of Oving which has among its attractions a pub (The Gribble) brewing its own ale and an impressively proportioned church.

ST. ANDREW'S CHURCH (8) is certainly roomy and uncluttered and has consequently been compared to a tithe barn. It provides an opportunity to view a variety of Victorian windows by different designers. We have designs by Lavers, Barraud & Westlake (quarried and pinkish), Baillie (bright non-realistic colours) and Dixon & Vesey (darker with thick black lines). There is also a Kempe window of 1901 in the south transept which is just about okay.

However pride of place must go to the 1881 main east window by Powells. This is a particularly fine *Faith, Hope and Charity*. The detailed drapery of the characters and the roundels above with their foliage and flowers are very Morris inspired but the window succeeds on its own terms. Henry Holiday may well have been the individual craftsman involved. Before leaving it is worth considering how wealth from the wool trade helped build such a spacious place of worship. *The church is open most days.*

THE FAITH' HOPE AND CHARITY WINDOW IN OVING CHURCH - PHOTO BY AUTHOR

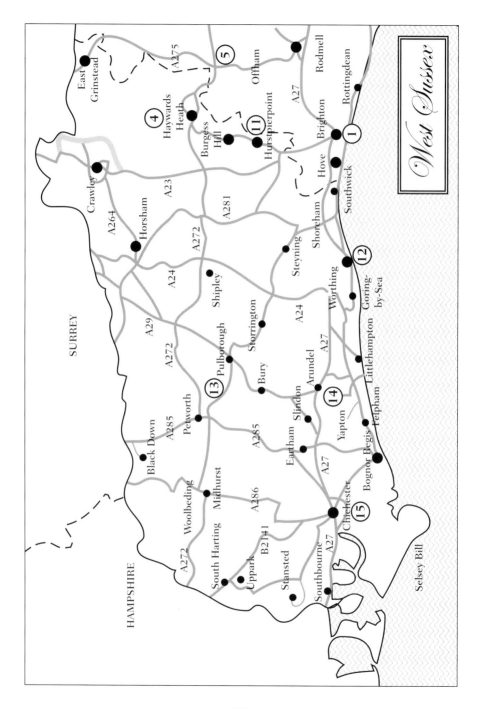

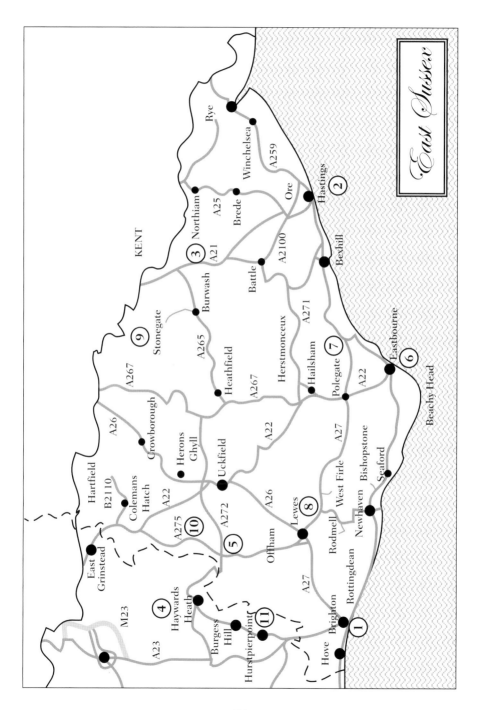

East Sussex

Further Reading

Barringer, Tim, *The Pre-Raphaelites*, (Weidenfield and Nicolson,1998).

Burne-Jones, Georgiana, *Memorials of Edward Burne-Jones,* 2vols. (Macmillan, 1904).

Hunt, William Holman, *Pre-Raphaelitism and The Pre-Raphaelite Brotherhood,* 2vols. (London,1905).

Millais, John Guille, *The Life and Letters of Sir John Everett Millais,* (Methuen, 1899).

Parris, Leslie, *The Pre-Raphaelites,* (Tate Gallery, 1984).

Prettejohn, Elizabeth, *The Art of the Pre-Raphaelites,* (Tate, 2000)

Rossetti, William Michael, *Pre-Raphaelite Diaries and Letters,* (Hurst and Blackett, 1900).

Thompson, Paul, *The Work of William Morris,* (Oxford University Press, 1967).

Wood, Christopher, *The Pre-Raphaelites,* (Weidenfeld & Nicolson, 1981).